More Praise for *Fitness After 40: How to Stay Strong at Any Age*

"Dr. Wright not only has a high IQ but also a high EQ, or emotional quotient. *She understands people.* Using her expertise as an orthopaedic surgeon, re-searcher, and masters athlete, she guides and encourages readers to live their best lives now. *Fitness After 40* is a must-read for everyone wanting to take control of their bodies through fitness."

—Freddie H. Fu, M.D.,
President of the American Orthopaedic Society for Sports Medicine;
and Chairman, Department of Orthopaedic Surgery, University of Pittsburgh

"Read this book! Vonda Wright's passion for life and boundless energy pour out of the pages of *Fitness After 40* as she teaches how to own your future through fitness. Join her patients and program participants as they learn her well-rounded approach that focuses on flexibility, aerobic exercise, carrying a load (resistance training), and equilibrium/balance training. As a Certified Athletic trainer, I have rehabilitated athletes and put them back in the game for more than 35 years. I would recommend *Fitness After 40* for all people with the desire to get back into the game, and the practitioners who care for them."

—Marje Albohm, M.S., ATC,
President of the National Athletic Trainers Association

"As a busy executive and avid ultra-marathoner, injury was the last thing I wanted to slow me down. Like many masters athletes, however, I found myself looking injury in the eye. When I first met Dr. Wright, I learned that she does not believe arriving at an arbitrary age requires us to simply accept injury or slow down. Her 'can do' approach inspired me to continue being competitive and the best I can be. In *Fitness After 40,* she gives great incentive and practice methods for setting and achieving fitness goals while minimizing injury . . . whether, for the first time in years, you are just stepping onto the trail or maximizing your com-petitive edge."

—Roger Oxendale, CEO,
Children's Hospital of Pittsburgh of UPMC; and Ultramarathoner

"*Fitness After 40* by Dr. Vonda Wright and Ruth Winter is a book of utmost importance as more and more of the population pass that age mark. In fact, a number of ski facilities no longer give a reduced rate to senior skiers because there are so many of them. One major problem I see in my clinics in Colorado is that often mature athletes may sit around all spring and summer, and then take to the ski slopes in winter. Because they have not remained active and are out of condition, they are very vulnerable to injury. *Fitness After 40* has excellent information about conditioning. Mature people not only benefit their mind and body by keeping in shape, they have fun and tend to keep their sense of humor. As 101-year-old Ben Levinson observed when he competed at the 1998 Nike World Masters Games in Portland, Oregon: 'At my age, just being anywhere is great!' Incidentally, I am now over 40, and mountain-bike ride, ski, horseback ride, and play hockey."

—Gloria Beim, M.D., Physician for the U.S. Track Cycling Team;
and Physician for the U.S. Team at the 2004 Olympic Games in Athens,
and practices orthopaedics at Alpine Orthopaedics Sports Medicine
and Hand Center in Crested Butte, Gunnison, and Telluride, Colorado

"In their new book, *Fitness After 40,* Vonda Wright, M.D., an orthopaedist at the University of Pittsburgh, and science writer Ruth Winter, M.S., team up to offer a motivational and informative book that should get over-40 readers off their couches and exercising with a smile. I especially like Dr. Wright's acronym F.A.C.E., which stands for F (flexibility), A (aerobics), C (carrying a load/resistance training), and E (equilibrium/balance). This book should help encourage readers to make the most of their 40+ years by encouraging a more active lifestyle appropriate to each reader's physical state. It's great that *Fitness After 40* shows readers how it's possible to put in place a safe, individual, and customized exercise program that doesn't have to take up a lot of time."

—Jan Yager, Ph.D., sociologist; and author of
Work Less, Do More: The 14-Day Productivity Makeover

"In *Fitness After 40,* Vonda Wright successfully shows readers how to take charge of their bodies in a healthy and sensible way. As we age and approach mid-life, it's far too easy to slow down, make fitness and healthful eating less of a priority, and let nature take its course (and lead us to lose muscle mass and add some extra fat layers to our bodies). Vonda shows us we can fight fate by incorporating more regular, sustainable exercise and physical activity into our lives. She also explains how to eat in a way that provides us with key nutrients and adequate amounts of energy (calories) to not only support our workouts and help strengthen our bodies, but keep our minds working optimally. Vonda's book helps readers not only look better on the outside, but feel better on the inside."

—Elisa Zied, M.S., R.D., CDN, registered dietitian and spokesperson for the American Dietetic Association; and American Council on Exercise certified personal trainer

"In one's pursuit of wellness and health . . . fitness is always the foundation. Exercise is medicine. Dr. Wright delivers this concept in an exceptionally clear, fun, and realistic way. *Fitness After 40* is recommended to all my patients of all levels because it's simply NEVER too late to start and get healthy!"

Marty Jaramillo, PT, "Physical Therapist and Trainer to the Stars"; Founder & CEO, I.C.E. Sports Physical Therapy; and co-author of *Men's Health Best Sports Injuries Handbook*

"As I approached age 50, I was overweight, had high blood pressure, and had not exercised in years. I decided it was time to invest in myself, and I worked hard following Dr. Wright's program for beginner exercisers. In the last six months, I have lost 40 pounds, I am more energetic and fit than I have ever been, and, best of all I am off high blood pressure medications for the first time in 10 years. Dr. Wright has a passion for getting us fit, and 50 is going to be a great year!"

—Linda, Pittsburgh, two-time participant in Dr. Wright's fitness programs

"Dr. Wright's twice weekly program for beginning exercisers has changed my life! After 12 weeks, I love to exercise and I believe I am physically capable of so much more than ever before. Last week I finished my first 5K race and I felt great. I am so excited to have *Fitness After 40* in my hands because it is like talking to Dr. Wright one-on-one. She takes care of my arthritic knees and encouraged me to take the next step and regain the strength and stamina I had let slip away over the years. I'm an athlete again."

—Mary Anne, Pittsburgh, Dr. Wright's patient and first-time participant in Dr. Wright's programs for STARTers

FITNESS AFTER 40

F I T N E S S A F T E R 40

HOW TO STAY STRONG AT ANY AGE

Vonda Wright, M.D., M.S.
Director of PRIMA™
(Performance and Research Initiative for Master Athletes),
UPMC Center for Sports Medicine, University of Pittsburgh

WITH *Ruth Winter, M.S.*

⁄AMACOM

AMERICAN MANAGEMENT ASSOCIATION

New York • Atlanta • Brussels • Chicago • Mexico City • San Francisco
Shanghai • Tokyo • Toronto • Washington, D.C.

613.7
WRI
18 –

3-10-2009

Special discounts on bulk quantities of AMACOM books are available to corporations, professional associations, and other organizations. For details, contact Special Sales Department, AMACOM, a division of American Management Association, 1601 Broadway, New York, NY 10019.
Tel.: 212-903-8316.   Fax: 212-903-8083.
E-mail: specialsls@amanet.org
Website: www.amacombooks.org/go/specialsales
To view all AMACOM titles go to: www.amacombooks.org

This publication is designed to provide accurate and authoritative information in regard to the subject matter covered. It is sold with the understanding that the publisher is not engaged in rendering legal, accounting, or other professional service. If legal advice or other expert assistance is required, the services of a competent professional person should be sought.

PRIMA is a trademark of University of Pittsburgh Medical Center.

Library of Congress Cataloging-in-Publication Data

Wright, Vonda.
   Fitness after 40 : how to stay strong at any age / Vonda Wright with Ruth Winter.
        p.   cm.
   Includes bibliographical references and index.
   ISBN-13: 978–0-8144–0994–7
   ISBN-10: 0–8144–0994–6
   1. Exercise for middle-aged persons.   2. Physical fitness for middle-aged persons.   3. Middle-aged persons—Health and hygiene.   I. Winter, Ruth II. Title.

   GV482.6.W75   2009
   613.7'0446—dc22
                                                                2008024322

Printing number

10   9   8   7   6   5   4   3   2

CONTENTS

"We are at a crossroads in our nation. We are standing at the corner of health and disease. Are we going to sentence ourselves to being a society defined by obesity and disease? Or are we going to choose to be a nation of health and vitality?"

**—Richard Carmona,
former Surgeon General of the United States**

FOREWORD

When I was 10 years old and playing pick-up ball with friends, I never dreamed I would be playing in the majors, let alone playing into my 40s. As a kid, I had no concept of physical conditioning. But the longer I played, the more I realized the importance of physical fitness for maximizing my career. Fitness became one of the keys to my longevity in baseball.

In *Fitness After 40*, Vonda Wright, MD, MS, with Ruth Winter, MS, have given you a way to maximize fitness after the age of 40. You really have no excuse for not staying fit, no matter what your condition is. Even old injuries are no excuse for letting yourself slide through the second half of your life unfit. I have chronic knee problems, for example, and in 2002, because of my hereditary history, I had heart surgery—yet I am still active. Aging affects athletes of all levels, from the professional to the person just getting off the couch and becoming fit. Aging, however, is not reason for slowing down. Even with the chronic aches and pains that so often accompany aging, I found that maintaining an active life and a high level of fitness kept me ahead of the curve. The reality is that as the years roll forward, we must not only stay fit but be smarter in how we stay fit to avoid injury and maximize fitness.

Of course, my game has changed with time, but I believe my professional longevity, rapid recovery from surgery, and ability to pick up the pace of my daily life were all dependent on my ability to work out regularly and stay in shape in all phases of my life.

While I have been retired from playing baseball for more than a decade, my life has been very full and busy. I spend a great deal of time with my cattle ranching operation on three ranches in Texas, in Gonzales, Live Oak/McMullen, and Brazoria counties. I'm a limited partner in a branded beef company that markets Nolan Ryan Guaranteed Beef. I have been involved in the banking business, having formerly owned a bank in Alvin, Texas, and one in Round Rock, Texas. In 1995, then Governor George W. Bush appointed me to a six-year term as a commissioner with the Texas Parks and Wildlife Commission. I continue to serve on a number of boards. In addition, I have maintained a close relationship with baseball. In February 2008, I became the team president of the Texas Rangers. Previously, I had worked with the Rangers as a special assistant to the president and was also a special assistant to the general manager of the Houston Astros. I am also a principal owner of two minor league baseball teams: the Triple-A Round Rock Express and the Double-A Corpus Christi Hooks. Both of these teams are affiliates of the Houston Astros.

As you can understand, I believe that saying you are too busy to devote time to fitness is not a valid excuse. My wife, Ruth, who was my high school sweetheart, and I have always believed that staying fit should be fun and enjoyable. We walk together, play tennis, run with the dogs, and play ball with our grandkids. Being active has become such an integral part of our lives that it's never a chore.

No one would argue about the value of fitness to overall health, but being fit means different things to different people.

If you are an elite athlete reading this book, physical conditioning is the vital link to your staying in the game, and you will find methods described in *Fitness After 40* to make you the best you can be. If you are not a competitive athlete and yet want to be fit enough to meet the demands of everyday life without getting overly tired, *Fitness After 40* will help you in your pursuit. You never reach a point where it is too late to start getting active. No matter what you've done previously, you can improve the chance for longevity and quality of life by getting physically active. You can sit down and read *Fitness After 40* and then get up and get moving.

Nolan Ryan
Alvin, Texas

Nolan Ryan was a right-handed major league pitcher for a record 27 seasons. He also holds the career strikeout record, with 5,714 strikeouts, and the record for no-hitters, with seven. He was inducted into the Baseball Hall of Fame in 1999.

"He's soft and he's fat and he's wearing my clothes and he's getting too old and he was born on my birthday and I'm afraid if I stop running, he'll catch up with me."

—What motivates masters athletes,
according to a popular Nike poster

INTRODUCTION

I wrote this book with one goal in mind: to empower you in the best half of your life to take control of your body and master how it ages. No matter what your age or ability level, you were designed to move, and it is never too late to start. Now is the time to maximize your performance and fitness, whether this means simply taking your first steps off the couch or ramping up to win your race age division. Your tool is exercise and sound fitness principles. We want to keep you in the game if you are active or get you into the game now if you are not.

If you have picked up this book, you are at least thinking about what living a fit life would be like. No more huffing and puffing on the stairs; no more longing for energy. You would feel vigorous and have the oomph to do the things you want, not to mention looking strong in your clothes. Living this life starts from the inside out, and the key is fitness through exercise.

I want you to understand—before you think I am simply another workout cheerleader in an orthopaedist's clothing—that I realize there can be real barriers on the road to healthy aging. I understand being busy, getting pulled in 20 directions at once, having family obligations, and dealing with financial constraints. I understand the dozens of other very logical (and some not so logical) reasons my patients offer up every day in my office. Here are some of the top excuses I've heard from my patients—and my replies:

- "I run around all day. Isn't that enough exercise?" *No! Your heart rate must be elevated for a minimum of 30 minutes a day.*

- "I can't afford to exercise." *Turn off your cable and use the money to join a health club and watch TV there.*

- "I think about it all the time, but I don't know where to begin." *Read this book and get up off the couch.*

- "We have a treadmill and an elliptical machine, but they are covered with clothes." *That is the most expensive clothes hanger I ever heard of. You know what to do.*

- "Even though I haven't exercised in 20 years, I used to be a Navy SEAL and do incredible physical feats. I can't bring myself to start exercising like a beginner." *After 20 years off, your body is like a beginner's. Let's go.*

- "The dog ate my sneakers . . ."

One of my patients actually told me that his dog *had* eaten his sneakers when he'd run out of excuses for why he was still sitting on the couch. He was one of my favorite patients, and he said it with a straight face. For an instant, I considered him seriously before a smirk settled in and we both burst into laughter. He wanted to be one of those svelte older men who looked and felt younger than the age on his driver's license, yet he had not made a move to get there. The truth is that 78 percent of people over 50 years old cite exercise as the key to aging well, but only 28 percent are currently doing anything about it.

No matter what your excuse or excuses may be, the fact remains that unless you take the time to invest in active aging now, it is likely that you will be forced to take the time to deal with illness in the future. Therefore, let's just put some of the major exercise barriers out on the table and hash them out. The three most common exercise barriers in my patients are "couch addiction," injury, and osteoarthritis.

BARRIERS TO EXERCISE

Couch addiction. Am I serious? Well, not entirely, and yet the habit of spending our lives as couch potatoes is a serious threat. I understand the issue, the lure of sinking into the soft sanctuary of the sofa after a hard day of work. In fact, during the beginning of my residency, I specifically bought my couch with napping in mind. At the local department store, I took flying leaps onto the laps of couch after couch, seeking the perfect place to take my naps. After 36-hour work days, my couch was the perfect relief.

The problem is that too much of a good thing *can* kill you. According to some of our nation's top physiologists, physical inactivity is a serious health threat and will lead to premature disability or death in more than 2.5 million Americans in the next ten years. There are 35 common diseases that are made worse if people are physically inactive, including diabetes, high blood pressure, heart disease, and stroke. In addition, women who spend two hours a day in front of the TV have a 23 percent greater chance of being obese compared to women who do not. I wish there was an easy way to tell you how to break the habit of spending hours every evening sitting on the couch watching TV. You simply have to make a real commitment to "just do it!" (as the Nike advertisement says). If you are a hopeless TV addict, then outsmart the problem and make your living room a home gym.

Regarding other barriers to exercise, it is true that those of us over 40 who exercise, and even those who don't, face the increased challenge of injury and arthritis. The number of people suffering from these problems is exceeded only by the products on the market promoting pain relief. Yet these two real and troublesome barriers to active aging do not have to be barriers at all. My entire career is about teaching athletes and active agers over 40 to be smarter as they avoid being sidelined. I not only treat their injuries but work with them to prevent injury and move past the aches and pains of arthritis. I look forward in the following chapters to sharing some of the information I give to my aspiring and inspiring patients.

Fitness After 40, however, is not just about exercising: It is about awakening the champion—the winner—that is within you. It represents years of research (my own and that of other experts) that can mean the difference between simply letting the aging process master you as opposed to making the next 40 years the best yet. Many of the commonly accepted stereotypes of aging are simply the effects of a sedentary lifestyle, not about real aging at all! Getting older does not mean being worse. Yes, there are changes. The truth is that no matter how fit you were at 20 years of age, there is a new you after age 40. You are simply not the same person you once were. However, not only can you still feel the strength and vigor of youth: You can perform nearly as well physically—and perhaps even better—than you did 10 or even 20 years ago.

Based on my research with Senior Olympians and as director of PRIMA™ (Performance and Research Initiative for Master Athletes) at the UPMC Center for Sports Medicine, your best may be yet to come. Last week, a group of adult onset exercisers (AOEs)—formerly couch potatoes—finished participating in one of our 12-week exercise programs aimed at helping them get off the couch and finish a 5K walk/run. In our twice-weekly sessions, they received much of the same information found in this book. They exercised together twice a week and individually two to three times per week. To our joy, seven of the participants rose above their expectations of finishing the 5K race and actually medaled in their age divisions. Talk about feeling vigorous! There is nothing like raising the bar of your personal best to make you feel alive. These AOEs, like you, had the benefit of the experience and wisdom that comes with age. By putting aside their past excuses for not exercising, they took control and got into great shape.

THE GOOD NEWS AND THE BAD

There is good news and bad news when it comes to remaining or becoming active after age 40. The good news is that increasing numbers of people over 40 are seeking ways to remain youthful by exercising. A recent survey of baby boomers—those born between 1946 and 1964—conducted by ThermaCare Arthritis®, a company that sells a heat pack that becomes warm when applied to the skin, found:

- 40 percent were living healthier lives and were more physically fit than when they were in their 20s
- 67 percent felt 11 years younger than their chronological age
- 57 percent reported being more physically active than their parents were at their age
- 33 percent boasted that they could beat their children in at least one sport

The people surveyed were either beginning to exercise for the first time (that is, they were AOEs) or were continuing programs they were already doing (active agers and athletes).

The bad news is that as we age, our bodies change, and these changes mean we are more vulnerable to injury. Injury is the number one reason people stop being active and the number two reason (after the common cold) why people go to the doctor. These same baby boomer survey participants revealed that:

- 67 percent suffer from muscle or joint pain weekly
- 73 percent say muscle and joint pain is a bigger annoyance than making sure they remain physically active
- 69 percent claimed that they were willing to work through their pain to remain active

You will find as you go through this book that I don't believe in the mantra "No pain—no gain." My objective is to help you maximize your exercise efforts by smarter training while preventing the injuries that not only cause pain but keep you out of the game. If you do get hurt, I will give you tips on how to recover actively and without making things worse.

THIS IS ALL ABOUT YOU

Orthopaedic surgeons and other sports medicine professionals have done a tremendous job taking care of adolescent athletes, college athletes, and professional athletes. We have, however, virtually ignored the growing number of master elite athletes and senior athletes over 40 years old who continue to remain active and fit. (The term "masters athletes" describes a broad category of amateurs who remain competitive after college and into their 40s, 50s, and beyond. Their goals can include winning the whole race, winning their age divisions, or topping their personal bests.) I work with and study mature athletes and see their thrill when they are victorious in competition and their indomitable spirit when they are not.

As I learned more about this dynamic group of people, I found that they have different needs than their younger counterparts. If you are over 40, for example, you need to train differently. This is because although in your mind you still feel 25 years old, your body will respond and recover from injury differently than it did decades ago. Being more mature is actually an advantage in some endurance sports, such as running and swimming, but being smarter about beginning or increasing exercise and training is crucial. Adult onset exercisers and masters athletes alike also have an advantage over their younger counterparts as they are generally finished with their educations and have more control over their time and resources. These advantages, coupled with a desire to be the best you can be at every age, make the second half of your active life an exciting place to be. *The fact is that a 75-year-old athlete may still perform many times faster and be in better health than a sedentary 30- or 40-year-old.*

I believe there is no one-size-fits-all exercise program. Your exercise regime should be individualized for you around sound principles and incorporated into your current activity. This book will help you recognize the capacity of your own body, adapt the principles described, and develop a fitness routine that fits within your lifestyle and abilities.

You can do more than you think you can. You can be stronger and more fit when you use the techniques described in this book. It will take determination and work, but as you travel through these pages, you will be hearing the same words I say every day to my patients. I hope you will feel like I am right there with you, helping you achieve your goals.

Each chapter of this book ends with homework. Get started now.

H O M E **W O R K**

1. Take a minute to think about what factors have been keeping you from living the fit life that you desire. Write some of these barriers down.

2. Are there excuses that you have been using over and over again that prevent you from taking the steps toward fitness after 40? If so, write a few down.

3. Look over your two lists. Are these barriers and excuses things you cannot control, or are there things you can do now to clear some of them out of your way?

4. Identify one or two of the issues you raised above that you can change this week. Can you rearrange your schedule? Walk to work or to the store instead of drive? Take the clothes off your exercise equipment at home?

ACKNOWLEDGMENTS

I am a "big-picture" person. New ideas or a vision of what I would like the future to look like have never been in short supply. Taking these immaterial thoughts, however, and turning them into reality, takes a team. This is true whether I am working in my operating room taking care of patients, executing the PRIMA programs for maturing athletes, or in the writing of this book. As I step back to appraise the completion of this project, I realize that I have many contributors to whom I am very grateful.

Of course, I must thank God and my family. God for giving me a mind capable of invention, and the hands to make it happen. My parents, Gene and Joy Wright, raised me to believe that anything I wanted to do was possible. I am most thankful for my precious blessing, Isabella, who is sweet and adventurous, and motivates everything I do now.

I thank Ruth Winter, my coauthor, for responding to my cold call and embracing, with great enthusiasm and diligence, the concept for this book. I am also thankful for her experience that guided me through the literary forest, one that is so different from medicine. We are both thankful to her son, Grant Winter, President of Manhattan Bureau Video Films, for his input and production of my media packet. Ruth would like to thank her husband, Arthur Winter, M.D., for his support. I thank Ruth for introducing me to Linda Konner, our fabulous literary agent, who courageously championed our proposal to publishers, and skillfully guided me through the process. Like a surgeon, she is both tough and compassionate; I like that.

I thank AMACOM for bringing *Fitness After 40* out of my office and to the world. Specifically, I thank Robert Shuman, our Editor, for his work on the manuscript, and for being the cohesive force that combined all the elements of this book. I am thankful to the AMACOM team: Mike Sivilli, our Associate Editor, for expertly managing the details of the manuscript preparation; sales representative Alan Trask; Irene Majuk, for charging forth with PR; and Cathleen Ouderkirk, Creative Director, for their hard work in envisioning how this book should be presented visually; and the army of behind-the-scenes people at AMACOM, whom I never had the privilege to meet, but who worked diligently on this book.

Special thanks to Chad Biddinger, masters sprint tri-athlete, and Laura Petrilla, our photographer. Chad is the founder and CEO of the premier racing website, www.racenation.com, and was the excellent demonstrator of most of the exercises pictured in *Fitness After 40.* Laura (www.laurapetrilla.com), lent her creative eye to capturing our words in pictures.

Studying Senior Olympians and maturing athletes is both fascinating and inspiring. I am thankful to the National Senior Games Association for allowing me access to their remarkable athletes during the 2001 and 2005 games, and to the more than 3,000 Senior athletes who participated in our studies. Also, I cannot forget the guidance of Peter Z. Cohen, M.D., who first turned me on to the Senior Olympics, and the team of researchers from the University of Pittsburgh: Dr. Jay Irrgang,

Kim Francis, Dr. Molly Vogt, and Gary Heinrich for their thousands of hours of work.

Finally, I must thank my Chairman, Dr. Freddie H. Fu, and my colleagues at the UPMC Center for Sports Medicine who helped me turn my vision for a Performance and Research Initiative for Master Athletes (PRIMA) into a thriving venue for maturing athletes of all skill levels. Through our PRIMA programs, PRIMA START and PRIMA Athlete, we assist these remarkable people to raise their performances to the next level while minimizing injury. Specifically, I appreciate the expertise of Ron De'Angelo, our performance director; Kathleen Nachazel, our program coordinator; and Karen Quinn, my assistant, for truly putting feet on these programs and keeping them moving.

Fitness After 40 captures the conversations I have with my patients daily. My patients inspire me to keep thinking of new ideas and to always strive to be a better surgeon. It is a privilege to be their doctor.

—Vonda Wright, M.D.

FITNESS AFTER 40

"Youth, large, lusty, loving—youth, full of grace, force, fascination. Do you know that Old Age may come after you with equal grace, force, fascination?"

—From *Leaves of Grass* by Walt Whitman

CHAPTER ONE

Healthy, Vital, Active, Joyful . . . You

Healthy, vital, active, joyful. These are not adjectives generally ascribed to aging, yet today, new generations of mature athletes and adult onset exercisers (AOEs) are changing the very paradigm of becoming older. They are not satisfied with a superficial, plastic veneer of youth but are remaining youthful on the inside—as well as the outside—by living actively. In fact, those who push themselves to the next level through competition report that they are more mentally and physically healthy than their sedentary counterparts. Mature athletes and AOEs are a remarkable and growing group of people. These vital sports enthusiasts exhibit persistently high levels of functional capacity as well as a good quality of life. They are not waiting for age to overtake them; they are proactively taking the steps toward maturing to perfection.

It never occurred to me that I was meant to slow down as one birthday passed after another. Even though I am now over 40, I still feel that thrill of competition and rush of adrenaline when I stand on the infield during a masters track meet and watch powerful athletes surge by, their faces being the only indication of their age. When I was nearing my 40s, I trained harder and became faster than ever—which may be one of the reasons I know firsthand that no arbitrary stage of life destines us to be on the sidelines.

REAL-LIFE INSPIRATIONS

Since I began to work with mature athletes and watch the National Summer Senior Games, also known as the Senior Olympics—a biannual competition of a cross-section of ordinary and elite senior athletes (age 50 to 100 years) who compete in 18 different sports—it has been a privilege and inspiration to know athletes such as 71-year-old Cliff Eggink, the original "Irongeezer." Irongeezers range from baby boomers to ultraseniors, some of whom are in their 80s and 90s. Far from being cranky couch potatoes, these people have a passion for physical activity and involvement in a healthy lifestyle. They have a dash of "iron" for strength of mind and body to maintain hale and hardy lifestyles amid an ever increasing, slothful, unfit population.

"At 61 years," Cliff says, "I started trying to be healthy. I stayed off the medication and got out of the couch-potato syndrome. Then everything just evolved. I had to push myself." Cliff did push himself. In 2005, at age 68, he was the oldest participant in the Ironman Arizona Triathlon competition. An Ironman Triathlon is 2.4 miles of swimming, followed by 112 miles of biking, followed by 26.2 miles of running.

Cliff is inspiring as a competitive athlete, but so is my father, who just wants to be the best he can be for his physical and emotional health. My father, Gene Wright, a former high school principal and now an entrepreneur, says:

> With the exception of a ten-year hiatus, I have always run. It is a part of who I am. I'm like the rest of the crazy runners out there: rain, shine, knee pain, feeling strong—I'm out there, adding up the miles. I run because I enjoy it, because of the camaraderie of the people I meet at races, and because I love the results I get from being fit.
>
> I was starting a new business around my 40th birthday and I stopped running. Of course, I started to get plump (5'10", 195 pounds), was short of breath (a brisk walk wore me out), had a steadily rising blood pressure and heart rate, and generally felt sluggish. I didn't want to do anything. I had to get back in shape.
>
> Boy, was it hard to start running again: It was slow—I mean, jog and walk, with the emphasis on walk. It hurt, and I mean all over. It was frustrating. I felt panic and anger that I might not get it back. This was a far cry from my college experience of enjoyment of flying down the road and being exhilarated.
>
> Eventually—it seemed like forever—I became conditioned with two- to three-mile workouts possible. I became encouraged. I told myself, "keep at it, guy, it is

possible." I began to lose weight and got down to 170 pounds. I felt better. My heart rate became lower (now at resting it is in the 50s). Again, I felt alive and ready to tackle the world.

Now I run a lot of road races, about 20 per year, from 5K through the marathon distance, and thrive on the competition, the feeling, and the people involved. I average 30 miles of running per week, with strength training twice a week.

Today, I'm 69 years old. I am in shape. I feel great. I am healthy and happy. I continue to run consistently, stay conditioned, set personal goals, enter races, and enjoy the road.[1]

My father is just one of the many athletes over 40 years of age whom I know who is in great shape. Liz is an example of a woman who got in the game at the age of 50. Growing up, Liz was never an athlete. Although she loved sports and participated in gym class in school, like so many other young women in her generation, she was discouraged from participating in heavy physical activity because "ladies do not sweat" and "all that movement was harmful for childbearing." She did try to earn a degree in physical education, but nine credits and three children later, her formal physical education ended. While raising an active family, she earned her Red Cross Life Saving certificate and taught swimming for many years.

One day, Liz was attending a senior sports classic, when they needed more swimmers to compete. On the spur of the moment, she decided to enter the 50-yard freestyle. As she pulled herself through the water, she thought to herself, "What an insane idea it is to jump into competition. I may die from the exhaustion." When she found out that she had won, she was surprised and delighted. Her spontaneous decision to jump in and swim the 50-yard freestyle led Liz to swim longer races. She won local and state senior swimming competitions and placed second and third at the 2005 National Summer Senior Games. She is no longer a slave to her aging process but has become the master of it.

Cliff, Gene, and Liz are not just exceptions but can be the rule for maintaining strength and improving performance through exercise. Today's mature athletes and adult onset exercisers have the potential to change the face and perception of aging in the United States. They are not bound to elderly behaviors in the same way as their parents. Today's athletes are unique; they are not merely sequels to their 20-year-old selves. They are highly active and motivated to stay young.

THE *FITNESS AFTER 40* Promise

If you are an elite athlete more than 40 years old, I can help you improve your performance. If you are a recreational athlete, I can encourage you to be your best and avoid injuries. If you are a couch potato, it is never too late to become fit.

In Chapter 2, you will learn exactly how your body becomes different and unique after you reach 40. The central section of this guide instructs you about all you need to know about the four components of fitness you must include in your daily regimen. You will learn about the easy-to-remember steps to fitness I call F.A.C.E.-ing your future. F.A.C.E. is an acronym I use to help my patients remember these four components of fitness after 40: flexibility, aerobics, carrying a load (resistance training), and equilibrium/balance. You will learn exercises that you can do at home, in the gym, and on the go to reshape your body, prevent injury, and become fit.

We will also examine the common barriers to your ability to stay moving, such as wear and tear and injuries that sidetrack us. We will discuss nutrition basics, how to set realistic goals, and strategies for establishing the critical mental edge you need for success. We wrap up with sources of information about fun and competitive athletic groups, good equipment, and organizations that offer access to specialized health professionals and resources.

Continue with me. Take the time to invest in your physical future by reading along with me and making a plan. You too can be inspiring—to yourself, to your family, to your friends, and even to those strangers who will wonder how you can be so fit after 40.

HOME**WORK**

1. Now that you have read about several inspiring masters athletes, think about yourself. What do you want your future to look like?

2. Close your eyes and picture yourself strong and buff.

3. Write down what you are going to look like and how you are going to feel. Be very descriptive. This will help you put feet to the direction we are about to go. Fitness after 40 is within your grasp. Just believe it and take action.

NOTE

1. Adapted from "Profile: Gene Wright—Fit and Fantastic," www.seniorsportsandfitness.com/genewright.html.

"We are indeed Masters, I told them. We are professors. We are professionals. We have come into maturity. And we have matured doing what appears to be childish things. Nevertheless our ability to live with questions and without solutions began when we took to the roads. Our belief in ourselves and in the living of our own lives developed through our running. It was running that released the treasures in our subconscious and gave us the creativity to put these treasures in substantial form. Keep running, I told the forties, fifties, and sixties looking up at me, the best is yet to come."

—Running enthusiast and writer
George Sheehan, M.D.

CHAPTER TWO

The New You!

*You Are Not Merely a Bad Sequel
to Your 20-Year-Old Self*

Step one in your project of investing in yourself is assessing where you are now and understanding what time and inactivity are doing to who you were made to be. You are not a hostage of Father Time. There are many ways to prevent your actions—or rather, your inactions—from robbing you of your youthful vitality. All it really takes is sufficient determination on your part. I hope to give you the knowledge and inspiration to feed that determination.

So how old do you really feel? Anyone who is older than the invincible 20s realizes that aging changes you. These changes, however, occur imperceptibly at the individual cell level, until you finally notice that time has passed and your body is not the same. You see yourself in the mirror and know you look different, but what is really going on inside?

My aim as an orthopaedic surgeon is to teach you about yourself and to demystify the mysterious changes occurring within. In fact, I believe that the better you understand yourself and the more information I can give you, the better decisions you will make. This is true for my patients and for you. What you are about to read is some of the very same information I give my patients every day.

DOES LIVING LONG MEAN SLOWING DOWN?

In a sense, your cells are immortal and ageless. They have the capacity to divide and renew themselves. As you age, however, this regeneration capacity slows; your tissues become stiffer and perform less efficiently. There are many examples in nature, from insects to humans, of decreased performance with increased age. Because of this overall slowdown, your physical prowess changes over time. But what part of slowing down is the result of inactivity, and what part results purely from the biology of aging? Is there a constant biologic rate of decline in your physical abilities independent of any additional health factors?

HOW FAST DO WE AGE?

To answer the question of how fast we age, we need to look at people who are models of healthy musculoskeletal aging such as the Senior Olympians. These athletes maintain a high level of functional capacity and quality of life throughout their life spans and may represent the truest measure of pure biologic aging without the variable of disuse.

So I pose the question again: What part of slowing down is accredited to the inescapable effects of biology? To find an answer, I analyzed track athletes, aged 50 to 85, who were participating in the 2001 National Summer Senior Games. (The results were published in the *American Journal of Sports Medicine* in March 2008.) As expected, with age, running times slowed somewhat in all distances from the 100-meter dash to the 10,000-meter run. Performance decline was slow and linear until people reached the age of 75, when the time it took for them to run their given distance (100 meters to 10,000 meters) increased sharply, indicating that performance was dropping precipitously. When I discussed these findings with the senior Olympians, they said they recognized the change. Many thought, however, that it was just their own performance that had changed with time—not the performance of all athletes their age.

Each year from age 50 to 75, performance times slowly crept up by less than 2 percent per year. When race times are plugged into statistical tests, the differences between runners at different ages were not significant until we reached the 75-year-old age group. At this point, the rate of decline per year increased to almost 8 percent per year. (See Figure 1.)

In track athletes, then, performance times are well maintained until age 50 and then modestly decline until 75, at which point

Figure 1. Change in performance with age for Senior Olympians.

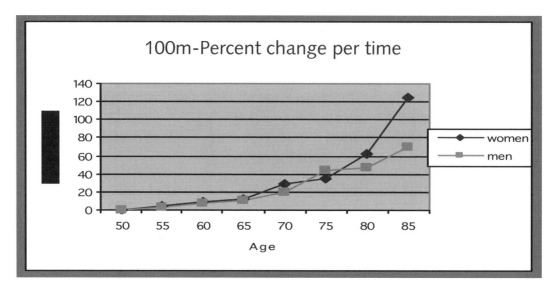

Source: Vonda J. Wright, MD and Brett C. Perricelli, MD, "Age-Related Rates of Decline in Performance Among Elite Senior Athletes," *American Journal of Sports Medicine,* March 2008.

performance becomes markedly slower. This finding suggests that if disuse and disease are eliminated as contributing variables, you should be able to maintain a high level of functional independence until at least 75. The loss of independence before age 75, therefore, is most likely the result of disease, disuse, genetic predisposition, or destructive lifestyle habits.

Although 75 looks like it is a line in the sand for athletic performance, this does not stop the Senior Olympians. It is not uncommon for competitors to run into their 90s and stand on the medal stand as proudly as anyone their junior.

Unfortunately, I also see the ravages of a sedentary lifestyle in my patients. I have had many chronologically younger patients (in their 50s and early 60s) who appear and feel old before their years. Research has shown that sedentary people decline twice as fast as their active counterparts.

Jim is a 51-year-old accountant. At 5′9″, he has a large belly (a big risk factor for heart disease and diabetes) and admitted that although he had been an athlete in college, the only exercise he got now was walking to the men's room and the company cafeteria. He came to see me because he had neck and back pain, which he attributed entirely to his occupation. In addition to their musculoskeletal problems, Jim and other inactive patients typically have high blood pressure, obesity, and type II diabetes, and become short of breath after simple activities. I treat their immediate orthopaedic problems, but I also encourage them to take the time to make a daily investment in their health by becoming physically active. I emphasize that when they are older and perhaps disabled, they will surely look back at the missed opportunity they have now for prevention.

One of the most satisfying aspects of my practice is when I convince Jim and the many others like him to get off the couch and invest daily in their physical health by becoming active. At times there are barriers to people becoming active, but often people just need some encouragement, education, hand holding, or even a swift kick in the right direction to start down a path that will benefit them greatly. I began a program for my patients that does all four of these things. PRIMA™ START is a program for adult onset exercisers or people getting back into the game after a long break. It takes people from the couch to a 5K walk/run in 12 weeks. Through twice weekly meetings and group exercise sessions, many of my patients have lowered their body fat, increased their fitness level, learned the components of well-rounded fitness after 40, and set and achieved fitness goals for the first time in years!

It is interesting to observe the difference physical activity can make in the lives of my patients. It always makes my day to see patients like Rita, a tall, slim, 45-year-old caterer who whisked into my office. She regaled me with tales of her last run, bike, and swim with great enthusiasm. She came to PRIMA™ with the goal of getting rid of her knee pain so she could compete in an upcoming marathon. Often I glance over the medical histories of patients like Rita only to find that, even in their 60s and 70s, they are taking no medication. If they have ever been hospitalized, it was years ago when they had their children. This is very different from the histories of my patients who have lived sedentary lives. Such people usually have suffered from health problems beginning in their late 40s or 50s, including high blood pressure, high cholesterol, and (depending on their weight) the onset of diabetes. All of these health problems can be modified with daily exercise, which is why I spend so much time talking to my patients about fitness. It is really the best way to control some aspects of your future health.

AGE-RELATED FACTORS

Your first step in becoming physically fit is understanding the multiple age-related factors—such as heart, lung, and muscle strength—that can contribute to your ability to care for yourself and your family as well as participate in athletics. The factors include:

- Your ability to train intensely, your reaction time, and your joint mobility
- Your skeletal size
- Your body fat composition

- Your anaerobic and aerobic power supply
- Your ability to recover
- Your strength, endurance, and coordination

Let's consider several of these factors.

ENDURANCE CAPACITY: IT'S ALL ABOUT OXYGEN

As you are reading this, hold your breath. It will be easy at first, but as you flip the pages, you will begin to feel the involuntary hunger for air, which is triggered by your brain stem. This hunger will grow and grow until your body demands that you take a gasp of air. Your brain is serious about making sure that you get enough oxygen, and if you don't take a breath, it will make you pass out in order to override your voluntary withholding of oxygen.

Oxygen is just that important to every cell in your body. Without it, your cells can't make energy, and their metabolism is less effective. You switch from a highly efficient energy-making machine to being 16 times less efficient and generating a lot of lactic acid (which is what builds up in your muscles and makes you sore). Without sufficient oxygen, we perform less efficiently.

Getting oxygen from the outside air to inside your cells takes efficient collaboration among your lungs, heart, and the cells they feed. As you age, the efficiency of oxygen delivery, and therefore your ability to perform at a peak level, shifts. The changes in performance with aging are attributed to lower lactate threshold (the point of exercise intensity where the body starts accumulating lactate in the blood), lower exercise economy/efficiency, and lower VO2 max. VO2 max is the most important of these factors. VO2 max is the maximum volume (V) of oxygen (O2) available for energy production via the oxidative pathway (the highly efficient system of metabolism in which energy is produced). VO2 max is dependent upon your heart rate, cardiac output (how much blood comes out of your heart with each contraction), and tissue oxygen uptake. Reductions in VO2 max are believed to be the primary reason for a decline in functional endurance with aging. Interestingly, scientists believe that part of the decline in VO2 max is due to lower energy, intensity, and time spent in activity or training.

How does aging change the efficiency of your heart and lungs in delivering oxygen? Let's find out.

The Efficiency of Your Heart

What an amazing piece of engineering our hearts are! They are essentially complex pumps that are able to adapt our blood pressure, blood flow, and blood volume to provide our bodies with all the blood they need. Over 50 years, an average of 80 beats per minute (which is the average heart rate) equals 2.1 billion heartbeats. It is little wonder that our hearts change with age. As you grow older, your heart adjusts. These adjustments come with trade-offs, leaving your heart more vulnerable to disease and other problems. Your maximum heart rate, heart muscle contractility (the ability of cardiac muscle fibers to contract), and the amount of blood coming out of your heart into your body (called stroke volume) all decline with age.

In general, without a preventive program, your heart will simply not function as well once you get older. Here are some statistics:

- 40 percent of deaths in people age 65 to 74 are from heart disease. For those over age 80, the figure is 60 percent.
- In your 20s, the maximum heart rate with exertion is between 180 and 200 beats per minute. At age 80, it is down to 145.

- A 20-year-old's heart can output (pump out) 3.5 to four times as much blood as the heart's resting capacity. An 80-year-old can output only twice the resting capacity.

You can counteract or slow many of the changes the heart experiences by exercise, blood pressure control, emotional stress reduction, and diet. Improving your heart function is one of the main objectives of continuing to exercise or beginning to exercise after 40.

When blood pressure increases, our hearts adjust by pumping harder. This is because the arteries—the blood vessels that take oxygen-rich blood away from the heart and deliver it to our bodies—become stiffer and less flexible with age. This stiffening and loss of flexibility causes blood pressure to increase. Researchers have noted that the wall of the left ventricles of our hearts become thicker with age. This thickening allows our hearts to pump more strongly against the resistance of stiff arteries.

All these adjustments, however, leave our hearts more vulnerable. Our arteries become less able to respond to changes in the amount of blood pumped through them. Thus, blood pressure may be higher in older people than in younger people.

As a heart ages, it also becomes less able to respond rapidly to chemical messages from the brain. The result is that the body cannot exercise as long or as intensely as when we were younger. This shows up as shortness of breath with less work— a sign that oxygen-rich blood is not moving fast enough through the body because the lungs are trying to breathe in more oxygen.

The heart of a healthy 70-year-old has 30 percent fewer cells than the heart of a 20-year-old. When heart cells die, the other cells must stretch and grow to stay connected. An older person's heart cells may thus be up to 40 percent larger than a younger person's.

It sounds all bad, but it is not. Exercise can keep your heart younger and more efficient. My 69-year-old dad's resting heart-beat is in the mid-50s, compared with the average resting heart rate of 80. The more fit you are, the lower your average resting heart rate because your heart is more efficient and pumps more blood volume with each beat. This means that even at my dad's age, the exercise he has done keeps his heart in shape.

How Fit Is Your Heart Now?

One way to measure how fit your heart is right now is to look at the maximum amount of oxygen (VO2 max) your body is capable of taking up and using in your muscles. Oxygen use declines by 5–15 percent per decade after age 25. The greatest portion of this decline is the result of changes in cardiac output (the amount of blood that is pumped from your heart in one minute). As training levels or activity in general decline, so does the VO2 max. (Men and women have relatively similar rates of VO2 max decline.) This does not mean that the hearts of masters athletes do not adapt to high-intensity exercise: Hawaiian Ironmen between the ages of 58 and 71 show the same heart changes (lower resting heart rates, larger left ventricles, and higher blood return volumes) as their younger counterparts. (Note that the age-predicted heart rate maximum decreases one beat per year after the age of 10. Each year we age, our hearts are capable of beating less quickly. This is due to a slower time of contraction and a longer rest period between beats.)

The good news is that physical training can make your body's ability to provide and use energy from oxygen consistently higher by maintaining cardiac output. How much improvement in the ability to provide and use this energy depends a lot on how you exercise. Intense endurance exercise, performed throughout one's life span, has been found to cut the decline in VO2 max in half. Physical exercise begun when someone is older can lower the loss of maximum heart rate but cannot increase heart rate by lowering contraction time.

The take-home message of all this: Keeping your heart fit through regular aerobic exercise will help maintain the amount of blood your heart is able to pump out with each heartbeat and deliver to your body.

The Importance of Arteries

To understand why aging is so closely linked to cardiovascular disease—and ultimately to find the causes and develop cures for this group of diseases—it is essential to understand what is happening to your arteries during normal aging (that is, aging in the absence of disease). This understanding has moved forward dramatically in the past 30 years, according to Richard J. Hodes, MD, the director of the National Institute on Aging. He points out:

> While we know a great deal about cardiovascular disease and its risk factors, new areas of research are beginning to shed further light on the link between aging and the development and course of the disease. For instance, scientists at the National Institute on Aging . . . are paying special attention to certain age-related changes that occur in the arteries and their influence on cardiac function. Many of these changes, once considered a normal part of aging, may put people at increased risk for cardiovascular disease.

Arteries are the tubes that carry blood away from your heart to your lungs and to all the other tissues of the body. Arteries are made of muscle, and like other muscles in our bodies, they tend to stiffen with age. Stiffening or hardening of the arteries also accompanies a high-fat diet and smoking. In addition, as our blood vessels age, they become narrower. This causes the blood pressure to increase because the heart must work harder to pump the same amount of blood through a smaller space. The heart compensates for this by becoming bigger.

The hardening of the arteries makes the heart's job of pumping blood through them more difficult since hard arteries are narrower and more resistant to flow. Soft, supple arteries do not show up on X-rays, but hard, calcified arteries look like shadowy bone. It is not uncommon for me to take an X-ray of a person's knees and see an outline of his leg arteries coursing down his legs. Hardening of the arteries is not inevitable: Many studies show that exercise can make arteries more pliable. Supple arteries are not only good for heart health, but also keep blood flowing to the brain, and are good for sexual performance.

Your Lungs

Every athlete gets out of breath when he or she runs fast. How soon you start panting is a measure of your fitness.

I remember a patient named Donna. Overweight and out of shape, she had difficulty completing the flexibility exercises we were teaching her because she would get short of breath. As the weeks went by, however, her body adapted to the new demands she was placing on it, and she began walking around the track with less distress. Each week, she added a little more distance and gradually could finish a mile, then two, then three comfortably.

Getting the oxygenated blood into your heart is one component of feeding your tissue, but first you actually have to breathe air to get oxygen into your blood. This is the role of your lungs.

Moving air from the outside world to inside you is a simple matter of rolling downhill. What I mean by this is that oxygen will diffuse, or go where it is needed most, when it enters the small air sacs in your lungs. Thus, when air is breathed in, the oxygen "sees" blood in the body that needs it. The oxygen attaches itself to the red blood cells to be carried to the waiting tissue. Anything that makes the lungs more stiff (such as age, smoking, or asthma) therefore prevents oxygen from entering the lungs, which decreases delivery to the blood.

It takes more energy to breathe as you get older. This is because the amount of air your lungs can hold decreases by about 250 milliliters (about the size of a teacup) per decade. From age 20 to 70, our maximum breathing capacity (called vital capacity) declines by about 40 percent.

In addition, the elasticity (the give of the lung tissue) decreases. There is also a decline in the number of lung capillaries (small blood vessels) and the quality of perfusion (oxygen exchange). Essentially, your lungs get stiffer and hold air and exchange oxygen for carbon dioxide less efficiently. The number one thing you can do for your lungs as you age is stop smoking.

Your Muscles: The Strength of the Machine

It's all good to have efficient fuel (oxygen) delivery, but what your body can do with it, once the oxygen is delivered, depends on the integrity of your muscles. Age-related changes to muscles and tendons have a great impact on your activities of daily living as well as your ability to participate in sports. They affect a muscle's power (the ability to move quickly) and its overall strength.

The changes seen in our muscles as we age are largely the result of loss of muscle cells, decreased size of muscle fibers, and increased muscle stiffness. Most of the muscle changes seen with aging are caused by the loss of lean muscle mass, or sarcopenia. We lose lean muscle mass beginning around age 50. By age 80, we have lost 50 percent of our lean muscle mass. People who are sedentary lose 15 percent of their muscle mass each decade between ages 50 and 70, and 30 percent per decade after age 70.

Our age-related muscle atrophy results from the shrinking of what are called type II (fast-twitch) muscle fibers. These fibers, which are responsible for muscle power, actually may shrink by 30 percent. This may be one reason that aged sprinters have markedly shorter stride lengths (40 percent shorter) and require a significantly higher number of strides to cover the same distance as younger sprinters. Not only do we lose lean muscle mass but studies of sedentary 70- to 79-year-olds have found that the muscles actually become replaced with fat. This is all true unless we do something about it.

Muscles become harder to move and more stiff with age. Loss of water and maturation of the structural components of your tendons and ligaments will cause them to become stiff. This is due to changes in the muscle composition as well as the way the individual muscle fibers cross-link during contraction. Stiff muscles are more susceptible to muscle injury.

If you need more motivation to keep your muscles moving, Swedish and Finnish researchers biopsied a muscle that extends the knee (called the vastus lateralis) of 18- to 84-year-old male sprinters. They found that the sprint-trained athletes did experience the typical aging-related reduction in the size of fast fibers, which play a role in the decline in explosive force required for sprinting. The muscle characteristics, however, were preserved at a high level in the oldest runners, underlining the favorable impact of sprint exercise on aging muscle.

The good news is that old muscle has the capacity to grow in size, or hypertrophy, just as young muscle does. In a classic study of frail elderly people, Dr. Maria Fiatarone of Tufts University found that weight training (consisting of eight repetitions at 80 percent of the maximum weight a person could lift once, three times per week) resulted in a 5 percent increase in strength per training day. Other researchers found that untrained elders can increase their rate of muscle building after two weeks of moderate weight training. If even frail 90-year-old men can increase their strength, then you can too.

Disuse atrophy may be another reason we lose both type I (slow-twitch endurance fibers) and type II (fast-twitch power muscle fibers) over the years. High-intensity training in masters athletes leads to muscle hypertrophy (or growth) and increased size of type I and type II muscle fibers.

A study of masters athletes who engage in exercise for fitness (running, and swimming without weight training) found that they had muscle composition similar to age-matched sedentary people, whereas those athletes who also participated in strength straining (such as weight training) had muscle fiber composition similar to control subjects who were 40 years their junior. Other studies show that differences in muscle composition between masters and youth runners is also because of differences in training programs, with similar regimens resulting in similar muscle composition.

The point of all these studies is that exercise not only feels good and makes your muscles look more fit but that staying active helps your muscles actually regain or maintain their more youthful makeup.

In addition to caring for masters athletes, I also have a laboratory where we investigate muscle and tendon aging with the goals of finding ways to make aging tissues heal faster. In a recent lab meeting, my research partner, Dr. Fabrisia Ambrosio, and I, were discussing some recent experiments. It appears that aging muscle cells can be made to behave more youthfully by using simple rehabilitation methods such as electrical stimulation. Dr. Ambrosio found that when muscle stem cells are harvested from old mice that had previously been exercised using electrical stimulation (a very common current rehabilitation method that stimulates both the power and endurance muscle fiber types), these old cells began to act more like muscle stem cells from young mice. It is exciting to think that the fountain of youth could be so simple and that exercise could actually change the very behavior of old cells! Another collaborator, Dr. Yong Li, found that muscle stem cells harvested from the muscles between the ribs of old mice also acted like young cells. This makes sense if exercise keeps muscle cells acting young because there is never a time when the muscles between your ribs are not exercising and moving to keep you breathing. In our laboratory, it appears that exercise could be the fountain of youth. . . . all the way down to the cellular level!

The other day, I was about to see a patient with a colleague who specializes in trauma. I read something on the chart about a 70-year-old male involved in a motorcycle crash with shoulder pain. I paused as I walked into the room and met Hank, a man with muscles almost like Arnold Schwarzenegger's. In his retirement from his first career as a business executive, Hank had decided to make his second career staying at peak performance and health. Now I am not suggesting that we all have to look like Arnold to be fit, but I am suggesting that an intentional approach to health, and in this case musculoskeletal fitness, can maintain our physical function regardless of our date of birth.

EXERCISE ECONOMY: HOW IT ALL FITS TOGETHER

So far, we've seen that oxygen is being delivered and the muscles use the oxygen to provide power and endurance for motion. How much motion and the ease of movement produced are termed *exercise economy*.

Decreased joint motion, coordination, and flexibility contribute significantly to declines in exercise economy. As discussed, aged sprinters have markedly shorter stride lengths than their younger counterparts and may take up to twice the number of strides to cover the same distance. While part of this may be the effect of lost muscle strength and power, the other important component is joint flexibility. Connective tissue, such as ligaments and tendons, are inherently stiffer with aging. This is the result of an age-related loss of tissue water content and maturation of the collagen in ligaments and tendons. In addition, many systemic diseases can make these tissues stiffer. As a result, joint motion decreases. For instance, knee motion decreases with aging. It is 120 to 130 degrees when we are in our 40s and drops to 95 degrees in our 70s and 80s.

Maintaining supple tissues by paying attention to stretching and flexibility is very important. Simply put, flexible soft tissue performs better than stiff tissue! Flexibility also maintains the stretch/reflex response of muscle and thereby boosts speed. Finally, stretching may reduce delayed exercise soreness.

In addition to the areas we have already discussed, there are several other important physiologic changes that occur with aging. They include cartilage, bones, tendons, body fat, and the neuromuscular system.

Cartilage: Here's the Rub

Aging cartilage is a big problem in the general population, but it can be especially vexing for the masters athlete who has no time or inclination to be slowed down by the pain or swelling that often accompanies cartilage that is "running out." Keeping cartilage healthy is a real balancing act for mature athletes. Inactivity and disuse atrophy can decrease the health of cartilage, causing softening, fissuring, and potential mechanical compromise. On the other hand, high-energy, high-impact activity on degenerated cartilage can cause increased wear. If you are a jogger or basketball player over 40, you must take this into consideration by listening to your body and the pain messages it sends. Such messages tell you that you are tired, that there is a problem or damage, or that the soft tissue of your joint is inflamed. When you feel these signals, be smart and *stop or moderate* what you are doing. You will make no gains by ignoring the pain and continuing to abuse your cartilage.

Your Bones: Taking a Strong Stand

Bone is an amazing, dynamic organ that is constantly changing and remodeling itself over our life spans. It is the only organ that can heal without leaving a scar and change its shape based on the stresses it experiences. This works in both directions. When bones experience a lot of stress or load, they get stronger. When they are not used to doing heavy work, whether it is labor or exercise, they get weak.

Our bones are made of a dense outer cortex and a spongy inner matrix of boney arches and bridges called trabeculae. When we age, we lose a number of these trabeculae. After age 40, women lose bone twice as fast as men at a range of 1.5–2 percent per year. This rate increases to 3 percent per year after menopause. Loss of bone density can lead to frailty and disability because of fractures.

We recently conducted a study of bone density in senior athletes and found that many more women had normal bone density than weak bone. This held true in even the oldest female athletes, who were more than 80 years old. The prevalence of osteoporosis in female Senior Olympians was less than in the general population at any age. In addition, significantly fewer participants in weight-bearing sports had osteoporosis. This all goes to show that even in chronically exercising senior athletes, doing high-impact exercise such as running and jumping is better for your bones. (Of course, exercise of any kind is better for the bones than being inactive.)

Your Tendons: Keeping You All Connected

Tendons are the tough cords of tissue that connect muscles to bones. In fact, every muscle in the body has a tendon that attaches to bone. Tendons thus can be large in size, such as those around your knee joints, or small, like the ones in your fingers.

Tendonitis is a painful condition that leaves the tendons irritated, swollen, and painful. It is a common condition, especially in over-40 athletes. Essentially, this inflammation occurs as the tendon develops repetitive microtears. The pulling of the tendon between the muscle and bone is felt mostly at the tendon insertion site and at the junction of the muscle and tendon. Tendonitis results after excessive repetitive movement. Continued use without stretching causes the fibers to gradually become tighter. For example, if you play tennis, you may overuse the muscles of your elbow through hitting the ball repetitively. This strains your wrist flexors as they begin on the outside of the elbow. The most common parts of the body where tendonitis occurs are the elbow, wrist, biceps, shoulder (including rotator cuff attachments), leg, knee (patellar and quadricep), and Achilles.

Of course, the condition can vary with each person as it strikes the areas he or she uses most. Symptoms can vary from an achy pain and stiffness to the local area of the tendon, to a burning that surrounds the whole joint around the inflamed tendon. Typically, the pain is usually worse during and after activity, and the tendon and joint area can become stiffer the following day.

One of the most serious tendon problems is Achilles tendonitis and rupture (men in their 40s and 50s are especially prone to the latter). The Achilles tendon connects the three large calf muscles to your heel. You never think about the Achilles until the slow ache you feel in the back of your leg explodes like "someone shot me in the leg." This is literally what men come into my office saying.

Your Body Fat Composition: The Fat Hanging Around

If none of the cardiac, lung, or muscle changes motivates you to get off the couch and get active, certainly looking buff and fit should. Many of my patients are happy that their hearts and muscles are stronger, but they are elated when they look in the mirror. Often, after a few weeks of exercise, my patients comment that their clothes are fitting more loosely. Even before they see a large difference when they step on the scale, their body composition is changing to become more muscular and less fatty.

Body fat composition rises in both men and women with age, and thus the percentage of lean muscle mass declines. Typically, active men at age 20 have 12–16 percent body fat, which rises to 19–26 percent by age 60. In the same time period, body fat in women rises from 23–28 percent to 28–38 percent. As body fat rises, inactive muscles become infiltrated with fat, which leads to decreased muscle strength.

For more than 50 years, however, researchers have known that it is not only the amount of fat you have hanging around that matters but where it is hanging. If you carry fat mainly around your waist, you are more likely to develop health problems than if you carry fat mainly in your hips and thighs. This is true even if your weight falls within the normal range.

Why is fat so dangerous? Not only does fat serve as a place to store excess energy, but it also functions as a hormone-making organ. According to Dr. Robert Ross of Queen's University in Canada, fat produces many hormones that cause high blood sugar (resistin), high blood pressure (angio-tensinogen), accumulation of plaque and inflammation in our artieries, and regulates our blood lipids. Fat around our middles (visceral fat) is much more productive than peripheral fat (the fat under our skin), and is therefore much more dangerous to our health.

When you carry your weight around your waistline you are more likely to develop "metabolic syndrome." This is a dangerous condition where your waist measures greater than 36 inches if you are a man, and greater than 40 inches if you are a woman and you have two of the following four cardiac risk factors: high triglycerides (blood fat), high blood sugar, high blood pressure, and low HDL (the good cholestoral). Metabolic syndrome increases the likelihood of developing type II diabetes by more than 500 percent, increases your chances of having a heart attack by 300 percent, and dying of a heart attack by 200 percent. Get out your tape measures and measure your waist now, and then let's get out and do some exercise.

A study by physiologist Cris Slentz, PhD—exercise physiologist and senior research scientist at Duke University Medical Center—and colleagues published in *The Journal of Applied Physiology* is a prime example of the benefits of exercise alone. Slentz's study included 175 men and women between the ages of 40 and 65 in North Carolina. All were overweight, inactive, and had mild to moderate cholesterol problems. The study subjects agreed to the following protocol for six months:

- The first group (the comparison group) would stay sedentary.

- The second group would engage in low amounts of moderate-intensity exercise (equal to walking 12 miles weekly).

- The third group would participate in low amounts of vigorous-intensity exercise (equal to jogging 12 miles weekly).

- The final group would pursue high amounts of vigorous-intensity exercise (equal to jogging 20 miles weekly).

Participants used treadmills, stationary bikes, and elliptical trainers. (An elliptical trainer is a stationary exercise machine that allows for the same benefits as walking and running but reduce joint pressure and impact. They can be set on varying levels of intensity.) Those who exercised on the three types of machines were directly supervised or wore heart-rate monitors to check their workout intensity. They were also asked not to diet or change their diet during the study.

Before-and-after imaging scans of the belly were done to check visceral fat, which is the fat that accumulates around organs in the belly area. The results were as follows:

- Visceral fat rose by nearly 9 percent in the inactive group.

- Visceral fat did not change with low amounts of exercise (at either intensity).

- Belly fat dropped 7 percent, on average, in people who got a lot of vigorous exercise.

- The group that got the most vigorous exercise not only lost belly fat but also had a 7 percent drop in fat around their waistlines.

This study shows that exercise can decrease the most dangerous type of fat—the type that makes us look like we are a basketball on sticks. In Chapter 10, we discuss the apple and pear phenomenon of body composition. While there's little you can do to change the actual apple or pear shape of your body that you inherited, you can decrease the visceral fat as well as change the appearance of your body, muscle, and skin.

The Neuromuscular System: Exercising Your Most Important Organ

The mind-body connection refers to the way your nerves and muscles work together. A decrease in coordination, balance, fine-motor skills, and visual-spatial orientation, as well as an increase in motor response time and altered proprioception (the sense of orientation of one's limbs in space), are all age-related changes in the neuromuscular system. Regular exercise seems to slow the rate of decline in many of these pathways.

As you were reading this chapter, you may have nodded as you recognized some of the changes you feel in your own body. You are no longer a mystery to yourself! But let's put all this talk of slowing down into perspective. Remember the Senior Olympians we talked about earlier, whose times slowed by less than 2 percent per year until age 75, at which point their times grew dramatically longer? When you put those percentages into real performance times, you see that although performance slows, staying active and challenging the body with physical training can lead to remarkable functional capacity at any age. In 2001, the 50-year-old man who won the mile race at the National Summer Senior Games won it in 4:34! Let me repeat that: The 50-year-old winner ran the mile in 4:34! The 75-year-old male winner ran the mile in 7:00. Seven minutes is significantly faster than your average inactive 40-year-old can run a mile . . . if he can last a mile at all.

So now you know more about being an active athlete and exerciser after 40. You know that your body has gone through certain changes and that you have unique needs. Therefore, the important thing to remember is that many of the declines and changes seen with aging are more accurately attributed to a sedentary lifestyle or an incomplete approach to fitness and can be entirely preventable through proper training.

The take-home message here is that your body will change because of the biology of aging, but without the devastating factor of disuse, we are capable of remaining amazingly fast and functional as we age. Many of the changes popularly associated with aging are less the result of biology and more the result of the lifestyle choices you make as you grow older.

Let's make some healthy lifestyle choices together. In the next several chapters, I will help you apply this knowledge toward slowing the declines usually blamed on age. As a result, you will increase your vigor and enjoyment of life.

HOME**WORK**

- How has your body changed in the last 20 years?
- Are you bigger, smaller, stiffer, stronger, weaker?
- What could you do before that you cannot do now?

GET TO KNOW YOURSELF!

This chapter is packed with knowledge, but I encourage you to stop for a moment and get to know yourself. I encourage my patients to keep a card with the following current information so that they will know the parts of their health profile they need to work on. It also serves to motivate them toward change.

Weight

Waist measurement (measuring tape at the top of your hip bones)

Waist to hip ratio (waist/hip should be around 0.8 or lower)

Body composition (% body fat < 25)

Cholesterol levels (including triglycerides, LDL, and HDL)

Resting heart rate (taken when you first wake in the morning)

Blood pressure (should be less than 120/80)

Family history (know the diseases that have plagued your relatives)

Bone density (especially women over 50 and men over 70)

The solution to the problems posed by your changing body is not to give up and slow down. The solution is to take inventory of the changes. Decide which parts of your more youthful frame you would like to regain, and use the chapters that follow to make a plan to get them back.

Age does not require us to stop being vital. It requires us to be smarter about how we proceed.

"It is our duty to resist old age; to compensate for its defects by a watchful care; to fight against it as we would fight against disease; to adopt a regimen of health; to practice moderate exercise; and to take just enough food and drink to restore our strength . . . ."

—Cicero (44 B.C.)

F.A.C.E.

Your Future of Active Aging

By reading Chapter 2 and looking in the mirror, you may recognize the changes that can occur with aging. But don't stop there. The fact is that many of the changes you see and feel can be modified and reversed by a comprehensive approach to active aging.

This morning, I was talking to a man named Carl who is participating in one of my fitness training groups about how his training was going and why he was participating in the first place. He observed that although he had always tried to stay active, as he aged he was continually sidelined by a series of injuries. Start . . . stop . . . start . . . stop. . . . He could never maintain the level of activity he wanted because as he would ramp up his activity, he would get hurt again. What he liked about my approach, he said, was the focus on being a well-rounded exerciser and learning how to exercise in a smarter way to avoid injury. "Yes!" I practically screamed as I clapped out loud. He got it!

Many of the women in my program, like Merle, are in their late 40s and early 50s. At 47, Merle no longer recognized her body and finally had decided, now that her children were more independent, to invest in herself. I am very proud of her as I watch her in our weekly group exercise sessions since she has made a lot of progress. There was still some-thing bothering Merle, however. In the last several years she had tried many diets, but like so many women who talk to me about their struggles, she said, "I really don't eat that much, but no matter what I do, I just don't seem to lose the weight."

The fact is that if women wait to focus on fitness until they approach their 50s, they add another degree of difficulty to the process: menopause! Estrogen is a so-called catabolic hormone, which means that one of its functions is to help us burn and use energy stores. As estrogen walks out the door as women enter menopause, they are left with an intact storage function and less burning function. It takes less energy for daily maintenance and therefore less food intake. Unless women burn more energy through smart activity, they are not likely to make progress on getting control of their bodies.

WHERE ARE YOU NOW?

When I think about fitness, I like to divide people into four categories. This gives me an idea of where people are now and how we would like them to progress. Figure 2 summarizes the four groups. You should review this chart and think about where you currently are on the fitness scale.

I suspect that few of you reading this book are in the Frail category. If you are, keep reading because no matter what you are able to do now, your body is always capable of improvement. In a landmark study by Dr. Maria Fiatarone, men over 90 years old and living in a nursing home took part in a six-week resistance

Figure 2. Four categories of fitness.

Who	Current Description	Goals
Elite	Trains daily. Competitive. High health and fitness reserves.	Maximize performance. Prevent injury.
Fit	Exercises two to three times per week. Moderate health and fitness reserves.	Maintain and increase performance. Prevent injury.
Independent	Lives independently. No exercise. Low health and fitness reserves.	Begin to F.A.C.E. a future of physical wealth (i.e., a storage of physical reserves). Move to Fit level.
Frail	Performs basic activities of daily living. Can't live independently. No health reserves.	Maintain or improve basic activities of daily living. Increase strength and independence.

training program. Even at this advanced age, they were able to increase their strength and stamina.

You probably fall within the Independent group. If so, you are among the 78 percent of people over 50 who identify keeping active as the most important factor in aging well and yet currently do not invest daily in their physical wealth. A good way to think about this is in terms of storing up health the way we save money. Every day, most of us go to work and make money. We invest some of the money for the future. In the same way, we must invest in our physical futures every day. If you don't exercise daily, you may do all right day to day, but you are not reserving any physical wealth for a rainy day. You are essentially living physical paycheck to paycheck, and when you get sick and need to draw from your saved up bodily reserves, the bank is empty.

Don't despair! If you are in this category, I am excited for you! You have the most to gain from this book and can make the most significant changes in your health and performance. Your goal is to use the F.A.C.E. principles (coming up in Chapters 4 to 7) to create a plan that will work for you. We want to move you up to the next level of being Fit.

If you do purposeful exercise two to three times per week, you are among the 28 percent of people in the United States who are in the Fit category. You are living the dream of all the people who are Independent but not Fit. You will find much valuable information in the following chapters on how to maximize your performance and fitness while taking the necessary steps to remain injury-free.

If you can easily perform your usual workout, it is time to shake it up and challenge yourself. Perhaps instead of just finishing a race you can challenge those in your age group. If you are plagued by recurrent overuse injuries or aches and pains, I want to help you exercise more smartly so that you can keep yourself out of your doctor's office and on the road.

If you are currently an Elite masters athlete, winning your age division or placing in open competition, I am inspired by you! You are at the same level as the 50-year-old male Senior Olympian (discussed in Chapter 2) that I witnessed winning the mile sprint in 4:34! I refer to you often when I speak and hold you up as an example of the physical heights we can attain if we are not hindered by the ravages of a sedentary lifestyle. For you, the challenge is to maintain your high level of physical fitness while remaining injury-free. For you, God is in the details.

HOW TO F.A.C.E. YOUR FUTURE

Whether you are Independent, Fit, or Elite, your approach to mastering your age while maximizing performance and fitness must be multi-factorial and smart. My approach to fitness after 40 is to *F.A.C.E. your future*! F.A.C.E. stands for the four components of fitness over 40:

1. F—Flexibility
2. A—Aerobic exercise
3. C—"Carry a load," in other words, resistance training
4. E—Equilibrium and balance

F.A.C.E.-ing your future and being smart works! Here is a good example. Lee is an elite male triathlete whom I've known for years. Tall and muscular, he is intense and always talks with great energy about his sport (a combination of running, biking, and swimming) and what race is coming up. At 44, he felt and frankly looked invincible and trained with the philosophy "If a little is good, more must be better." Lee was consistently rewarded with top age group finishes.

At one point, though, he started to call me more frequently about aches and pains he had never had before. We would talk about his training schedule, how tight his muscles were, and what he ate. He listened and asked a lot of questions, and I told him repeatedly that he needed to modify his training by mixing up his mode of exercise, by working out intensely only every other day, and by instituting a flexibility program. The next time we would talk, though, he had not done any of the things I'd outlined. All his questioning did not make him smarter, and he had continued with his usual intensity, despite the fact that he was still hurting.

Almost on a whim, Lee decided to qualify for the Boston Marathon, which meant that he had to run a different marathon and finish within a specific time. Only one month before the first marathon, he jumped into an advanced training program, taking long runs of 18–20 miles, when previously he had run consistently but not at these high and intense distances. Again, he said, he thought that "If one 20-miler was good, several must be better," so he continued to pound the pavement.

Lee began to have pain in the front of his left leg, but since the first marathon was close at hand, he continued to train. On race day, he arrived late and had to start the race after the gun sounded. He made up ground by zigzagging through the slower crowd, jumping up on curbs to get around people. By the end of the marathon, Lee had qualified for the Boston, but the pain in his left anterior tibia (his shinbone) was tremendous, and it did not go away in the weeks following the race. Lee didn't have a simple shin splint or muscle strain. Lee had a tibial stress fracture. When he told me what he had done, it was all I could do to keep "I told you so" from coming out of my mouth.

If he had listened to my advice about F.A.C.E.-ing his future and being smart, Lee might have been able to avoid his injury. The increased road intensity and load of the marathon he had undertaken had overloaded his healthy bone. He was treated for a few months with activity modification, cross-training, flexibility training, and a running analysis. He was then diagnosed with hamstring tightness, quad/hamstring imbalance, and core (abdominal muscle) weakness.

Specific exercise regimes as well as methods for maximizing running efficiency were suggested. We used a series of core and upper leg exercises, executed with rubber exercise bands. PRIMA uses a "functional" approach to strength where resistance is applied through a range of motion instead of a weight bench. Functional training strengthens our muscles just as they work in real life. This allowed him to perform these skills anywhere, even when he was traveling on business. After allowing a period of activity modification, including water running, we introduced hard surfaces again in a slower and more gradual program. Lee's stress fracture has now healed, and he is once again building mileage for his next race.

F.A.C.E.-ing your future is not only for competitive athletes like Lee but is the foundation of fitness for people of all ages and ability levels. Keep reading. The following chapters will explain why each of the four components is critical to your future and will empower you to incorporate these components of fitness over 40 into your plan. Let's go! It is time to make a move.

HOME**WORK**

Look back at Figure 2 in this chapter. Identify which category you are currently in. Review the goals for your current level. Keep them in mind as we make a plan for your future in the next several chapters.

"The doctor of the future will give no medicine but will interest his patients in the care of the human frame, in diet and in the cause and prevention of disease."

—Thomas Edison

CHAPTER **FOUR**

F.A.C.E.

Your Future Through F—Flexibility

You and I know that remaining flexible is good for us. Focusing on flexibility, however, is my least favorite part of my fitness regimen, and you may feel the same way. Flexibility is easy to ignore, and many active people do ignore it. The truth is that by and large, the active agers and athletes who come into my office with repetitive injuries are stiff as boards! Their hamstrings, their calves, their shoulders, and their backs are all stiff. This perpetual tightness often leads to injury and frustration. These people are not limited by the number of years they have lived but by the length of their muscles. It doesn't have to be this way. You grew these muscles and you can make them perform for you in just 15 minutes per day!

Flexibility is the ability of muscle to lengthen and allow your joints to move through a full range of motion. Maintaining muscle flexibility increases athletic performance, improves running economy (decreased energy expenditure at a given speed), prevents injury, decreases soreness, and hastens rehabilitation following injury. In their relaxed state, muscles and the tendons that attach them to your bones are "crinkled" up. (This is literally the scientific term for their accordion-like resting state.) When they are in a chronically shortened state, muscles and tendons prevent our joints from moving through their full range of motion, which changes the way we walk, our posture, and, among other things, our golf swing (heaven forbid). Not only this, but stiff muscles and tendons are like the old dried out rubber bands you find in the back of your desk drawer. One pull and these brittle old elastic bands "pop." Muscles are elastic bands, and when stiff, they are also more likely to "pop" and sideline us with injury.

I have an elite masters sprinter named Ron who trains at our performance center. He is incredibly driven, and works with high intensity to explode down the track. I first saw him because he was having pain in his hamstrings (muscles in the back of his thighs responsible for powerful knee flexion). When I assessed him, I found that his hamstring muscles were tight like guitar strings. I would almost "twang" them with my finger as I flexed his hip and tried to straighten his leg into the air. This is a scary situation for any sprinter, but especially in a masters sprinter whose muscles and tendons are aging. Daily stretching was not a part of Ron's workout regimen. We talked for a long time about flexibility and the priority it should be for him. He was not F.A.C.E- ing his competitive future, but had continued to do the types of workouts he had done since his twenties. Unfortunately, he could not undo the years of progressive hamstring tightening overnight, and he ultimately injured his hamstring. He has been carefully rehabilitated back to competitive form, but paying attention to flexibility would have saved him a lot of pain and improved his sprinting.

Here is another example of what I'm talking about. You have all seen elderly people walking around with bent knees all stooped over. While there can be many reasons for this, one big reason people start walking with bent knees is shortening of the hamstrings. The hamstrings are the large muscles in the back of your leg that connect your pelvis to your lower leg. Hamstrings act as the rubber band that flexes your knee during walking or, more powerfully, during exercise. After years in a crinkled state, muscles like hamstrings get shorter. The thigh bone (femur), however, does not get shorter, so the only way you can make the distance between the pelvis and lower leg shorter is to bend your knees. Well, you can't walk with bent knees and straight hips, so to compensate, you bend your hips forward and, before you know it, you are walking around with a stooped gait—looking old.

Flexibility is essential in preventing all kinds of injuries but tendonitis in particular. Prevention of tendonitits requires stretching the muscle on a regular basis, which allows less pulling and traction on the tendon's attachment to the bone. When tendonitis does occur, it is important to treat it immediately and prevent it from reaching the more severe stage called tendonosis. Even if you have not reached for your toes in years, it is not too late to start stretching and regaining your flexibility. You can *F.A.C.E. your future through F (flexibility) in a mere 15 to 20 minutes a day.*

THE FACTS ON FLEXIBILITY

Here are the down and dirty scientifically proven facts for regaining and maintaining your flexibility. First, you must stretch every day. Yes, every day! When I say this to my patients, I often see a look in their eyes that says, "When am I going to fit this in?" To which I reply, "I mean it. Get out of bed, hop in the shower, get out, stretch for 15 minutes, and get on with your day. If morning doesn't work for you, take 45 minutes at lunch instead of an hour and use the other 15 to stretch. (Stretching usually does not break a sweat and require getting dressed again.) Or stretch in the evening while you watch the news or your favorite show." Stretching does not have to be done all at once either. You can break the stretching regimen up over the course of the day and do one body part at a time.

Changes in flexibility are dependent on the frequency and duration of stretching. For people under 65 years old, maximum benefit is achieved with a slow muscle stretch until the muscle feels tight but doesn't hurt. (Slow stretching lengthens muscle fibers without causing tearing and damage. This is important since muscle tears often heal with scars, which are very stiff.) Once you reach this place, hold the stretch for 30 seconds without bouncing. While any stretching is better than nothing, less than 30 seconds is less effective. After 30 seconds, rest for 10 seconds and then repeat the stretch for a maximum of four repetitions. No added benefit is gained if you hold the stretch for more than 30 seconds or do more than four reps.

The caveat to this is if you are older than 65. If you are, you need to hold the stretch for 60 seconds. This will gain almost double the range of motion. If you are younger than 65, there is no added benefit to holding a stretch for 60 seconds.

Perform the set of stretches only once a day. No added benefit has been found with more than one set per day for each muscle group. It takes about six weeks of consistent stretching to see good results, and then you must maintain your muscle length by continuing daily stretches. Studies have found that if you stretch for six weeks and then take four weeks off, you will return to baseline as if you had never put in the effort. The good news is that by starting over, you can regain your flexibility again . . . after six weeks.

THE FOAM REVOLUTION

"Go and buy a foam roller." These are words I say to most of my aging and youthful athletes alike. Foam rolling is a marvelous way to stretch your tight tendons and muscles. Essentially, this log of hard foam serves as a rolling pin to roll out and stretch your tendons, and is a great way to warm up for activity. I find this tool especially good for stretching hard-to-stretch tissue like the IT (iliotibial) band, which runs down the side of your leg from your hip to your knee, and the muscles of the leg. You lay on the roller and pull your body slowly back and forth across the roller with your arms. It might be a little uncomfortable while you are doing it, but it feels unbelievably good when you are done. Go to www.fitnessafter40book.com to view demonstrations of foam rolling.

In summary:

- If you are younger than 65, you should hold each stretch 30 seconds and do four repetitions once a day.
- If are older than 65, you should hold each stretch 60 seconds and do four repetitions once a day.

This means that it only takes about two minutes to stretch each muscle group each day and about 15 to 20 minutes for the whole body.

Two more things. While it seems correct intuitively, stretching one side does not increase the flexibility of the other side. You need to stretch both sides. In addition, static stretches—like the ones shown in the following pages—are more effective than dynamic or moving stretches.

The following pages present a simple and effective general plan for daily stretching. You should be able to accomplish this program in approximately 15 to 20 minutes.

NECK, UPPER BACK, AND CHEST

Many of us carry our stress and daily tension in our upper back and the muscle connecting our shoulders and neck (called the trapezius). The trapezius muscle can knot up and become so tight that it causes headaches in the back and sides of our heads. The following stretches and range-of-motion exercises should be performed daily and any time you begin to feel tightness in your neck and upper back.

Neck Range of Motion

Photos 1 through 4 shows the neck range-of-motion exercise.

Photo 1

1. Begin in a seated position.

2. Leading with your chin, bend your neck forward so that your chin moves toward your chest (Photo 1). You will feel a stretch down the back of your neck and across your upper shoulders.

3. Next, turn your chin toward your left shoulder and try to touch your shoulder with your chin (Photo 2).

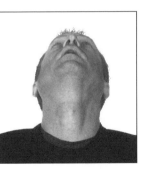

Photo 2   Photo 3   Photo 4

If you cannot reach your shoulder, don't worry. Don't raise your shoulder to meet your chin.

4. Extend your neck back so that your chin is facing the ceiling (Photo 3). You may feel pressure in the back of your neck and shoulder blades.

5. Finally, turn your chin toward your right shoulder (Photo 4). Again, do not raise your shoulder to meet your chin.

This range-of-motion exercise should be performed in a slow, continuous arc, so that you are moving your chin from front to side to back to side. Do four revolutions. You may hear some crunching in your neck as your head moves on your spine. Painless crunching is fine. However, if you have pain shooting down your arms or numbness in your hands when doing this exercise, stop and make an appointment with your orthopaedic surgeon to make sure your nerves are not being pinched.

Shoulder Roll (Upper Back/Shoulder Range of Motion)

Many of us sit hunched over a desk all day. We allow our shoulders to slide forward and our back muscles, between our shoulder blades, to become weak and lax. This eventually leads

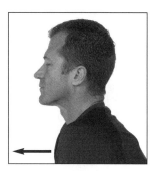

Photo 5 (shoulders forward)

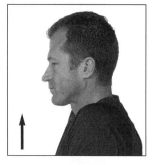

Photo 6 (shoulders up)

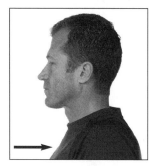

Photo 7 (shoulders back)

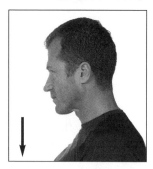

Photo 8 (shoulders down)

to a rounded shoulder posture, gives us upper back aches, and makes us look shorter. Do the following shoulder roll (shown in Photos 5 through 8) at least once a day and any time you sense that you are sliding back into a slumped shoulder posture.

1. In a seated position, let your shoulders relax.

2. Flex your chest (pectoralis) muscles by bringing your shoulders forward (Photo 5).

3. In a continuous motion, flex your trapezius muscles (between your neck and shoulders) by raising your shoulders up (Photo 6).

4. Finally, squeeze the muscles between your shoulder blades and bring your shoulders back and down (Photos 7 and 8).

When doing this exercise, keep your upper back muscles contracted and your shoulders back. Your chest should be raised with your shoulders in this position. You may notice that you are sitting higher in your chair, and it should feel great. Do this rotation four times, and then try to maintain this upright posture throughout the day. You may even want to stand sideways in front of a mirror and notice your improved posture!

As I was sitting here writing and performing this range-of-motion exercise, my right shoulder blade popped. Popping is fine unless it is painful or causes mechanical-type locking. Popping in any joint that is not painful usually represents simple movement of tendons or ligaments across the bones.

Seated Trapezius Stretch

Now that your shoulders are back and your upper back is straight, you need to stretch your trapezius muscle. See Photo 9.

Photo 9

1. Turn your chin toward your right chest.

2. Place your right hand over the top of your head and gently pull your head down toward the right (Photo 9). You will feel a stretch in your left trapezius, and if you touch your left neck with your left hand, you will feel the tight muscle being stretched. Hold this stretch for 30 seconds and then relax. Repeat this stretch four times, remembering to breathe.

3. Switch chin direction to the left. Place your left hand over the top of your head and gently pull down to stretch your right trapezius muscle.

You may want to vary this routine by moving directly from a shoulder roll (the previous exercise, done for upper back/shoulder range of motion) to a trapezius stretch: shoulder roll, trapezius stretch, shoulder roll, trapezius stretch, and so on.

Chest Stretch

You are going to hear me say this many times: *The key to the back is the front!* Usually, I say this in relation to the lower back and core, but even in the upper back and shoulders, we cannot forget to stretch our chest muscles. People who work out a lot usually focus on their pectoralis muscles and building a big chest. (Who can blame them? It looks great.) The problem is

Photo 10

that a chest that is tight and contracted only adds to the posture problems and back tension we were working on in the previous three exercises. So now, let's stretch our chests. See Photo 10.

1. Find a corner or doorway to stand in.

2. Raise your arms to shoulder height and bend your elbows 90 degrees so that your palms are against the wall and your fingertips are facing the ceiling.

3. Place your feet shoulder width apart and lean forward. You should feel a stretch across your chest. If you do not, then step back another step and lean forward again. Hold this position for 30 seconds and repeat four times.

SHOULDERS AND ARMS

Our shoulders and arms are the mainstay of our daily productivity. We do not realize how much we rely on them until even a small pain sidelines us or wakes us from sleep. The following stretches (coupled with the "Fitness to Go" shoulder section of Chapter 6) will take you a long way toward peak shoulder and arm performance.

Shoulder Stretch

With daily use, we usually do a good job maintaining shoulder motion to the front and sides. We do not do as good a job at keeping the back of our shoulders and rotator cuff (the four small muscles that keep our shoulder joint together) well stretched. Keeping the back part of the shoulder flexible helps our rotator cuff maintain shoulder stability. This is true for regular people like you and me as well as elite athletes such as baseball pitchers. Flexibility in the back of the shoulder is key to keeping your arm well centered in your shoulder socket. See Photo 11.

Photo 11

1. Stand with your feet shoulder width apart.
2. Raise your right arm up to shoulder height and move it across the front of your body.

3. With your left arm, pull the right arm as close to your chest as possible and hold it for 30 seconds (Photo 11). You should feel the stretch across the back of your shoulder.

4. Repeat this four times, then switch to the left side.

Triceps Stretch

Use the exercise shown in Photo 12 to keep your triceps (the muscle in the back of the upper arm) stretched.

1. With your feet shoulder width apart, raise your right arm straight up and over your head.

2. Bend your elbow so that your right hand is reaching for your left shoulder.

3. Use your left hand to press back on your right elbow (Photo 12). You will feel a great stretch in the back of your arm and upper shoulder.

4. Hold for 30 seconds and repeat four times on each side. Remember to breathe while you do this. (It feels great.)

Photo 12

Lower Back

"Oh, my aching back!" This complaint is shared by so many people. But what is the key to your back? Say it with me: *The key to my back is my front.* In the Fitness to Go section on the back in Chapter 6, you will learn exercises that will revitalize the strength of your back and core. Your core muscles are your natural weight belt. To find them, put your hand on your waist, then suck in your belly button toward your spine. Did you feel the muscles under your skin get tight? These are your core muscles. They run obliquely from your spine to the front of your body. If you were not able to feel these muscles, try bearing down like you are going to the bathroom. You should be able to feel them now. Everything we do begins with our core muscles. These are the top of the exercise food chain as far as I'm concerned.

Until we get to Chapter 6, though, what can you do now if your back is killing you? Lower back stretches will help, as shown in Photos 13 and 14.

1. Begin on your knees.
2. Place your hands in front of you on an exercise ball or the seat of a chair.
3. While keeping your back flat, reach forward with your arms and lower your buttocks to your feet (Photo 13). You will feel a stretch along the sides of your back.
4. Hold for 30 seconds, while breathing, then relax. Repeat four times.

Photo 13

Photo 14

5. Next, place your hands shoulder width apart on the ground. It will look like you are crawling.

6. Gently arch your back toward the ceiling and tuck your buttocks in (Photo 14).

7. Hold and repeat four times.

8. After the last arch, lower your buttocks to your heels with your arms stretched out front and let your back relax.

HIPS AND LEGS

There are many ways to accomplish a stretch. You may have learned to stretch your legs in many different ways as you worked with different coaches. The following hip and leg stretches will give you a general approach to the lower body. Remember, as always, hold each stretch for 30 seconds, repeat four times, and never bounce. If you find you are having difficulty balancing during these stretches, read Chapter 7 on regaining your equilibrium, and perform these stretches with something to hold on to nearby.

Hip Flexor Stretch in Three Planes

1. Start by standing with feet together.

2. Step forward onto the right leg while keeping your knee aligned above your ankle and your hips forward.

3. Raise both of your hands above your head as you lean forward. You should feel a gentle stretch in the front of your back leg.

4. Then, lean toward the right leg and raise your left arm over your head. The stretch will move to include your left side as well as the front of your back leg.

5. Finally, raise your left arm above your body and twist it to behind your body. This opens up the left side of your body.

6. Hold each position for 30 seconds, and then switch legs and repeat all three positions.

7. Repeat the rotations four times.

Holding your legs in a lunge like this for 90 seconds (30 seconds in each position) may initially be too much for you. That is fine. Work up to it.

Hamstring Stretch

At any age, the hamstrings are commonly damaged if flexibility is not maintained. They are powerful and cross the hip joint as well as the knee joint, driving hip extension and knee flexion. This leaves them vulnerable to injury when our explosive athletic demands overcome their flexibility.

The hamstring stretch can be performed lying on the ground as shown in Photo 15 or may be as simple as raising your heel up on a stool or chair and leaning forward. I do my personal favorite variation after I run. While still out in the park or street, I place my feet a little more than shoulder width apart and lean forward with a straight back from the waist. With my knees straight, I place my palms on the ground, which gives me a great stretch in the back of my legs. To increase the stretch, all I have to do is move my feet closer together until, when I'm really flexible, my feet are together and my palms are on the ground.

Years ago, when I was a ballet dancer, I loved to do hamstring stretches in the following way:

1. Lay down with the small of your back against the floor.
2. Bend your left knee to 90 degrees to stabilize your hips.
3. Slowly raise your right leg off the ground with the knee as straight as possible. Your right hip should not rise off the floor and the motion should be coming only from your hip (Photo 15).
4. As your foot approaches vertical, you will feel a stretch in the back of your leg.
5. Hold your leg in this raised position for 30 seconds. As you become more flexible, your foot and knee will come past vertical and get closer to your chest and ear. (It's true. That is why I loved this stretch as a dancer.)
6. You can modify this exercise by placing a towel around the sole of your shoe and pulling your leg back toward your chest with a straight knee.
7. After 30 seconds, relax your knee and then repeat three times before switching to the left leg.

Photo 15

Quadriceps Stretch

If you were in my office with knee pain, you would hear me say, "The quads are the key to the knees!" The quadriceps—a giant set of four muscles (thus the name quads) in the front of the legs—are powerful knee protectors. They also cross two joints—the hip and knee—and are responsible for some hip flexion and all knee extension. They also are key in absorbing the shock of our body weight across the knee and for keeping our kneecaps aligned down the center of the knee. Learn the quad stretch shown in Photos 16 and 17 and pay special attention to the Fitness to Go section of Chapter 6 on knees.

1. Stand with feet together and hips straight.

2. Bend your right knee back and take the front of your right foot in your right hand.

Photo 16   Photo 17

3. Keeping your knees even (i.e., do not let your right knee swing forward), bend your right knee back. You will feel a stretch in the front of your leg from above your hip to your knee. Do not allow your posture to curve forward but keep standing straight up.

4. Hold the stretch for 30 seconds and then relax.

5. Repeat this four times and then switch to the left quad.

The Calves

We finally have made it down the entire body and you should be feeling loose and great, perhaps even a little tired since stretching

Photo 18   Photo 19

can be hard work. But we're not done yet: We can't forget our calves. They are important in every step we take and look really great when they are in shape. The calves are actually made up of two muscles: the gastrocnemius, which crosses the knee and ankle, and the soleus, which crosses only the ankle. The ends of the gastroc and soleus tendons fuse in the lower part of the leg as the Achilles tendon. Keeping the calves flexible is not only important for preventing calf tears but for preventing the ever troublesome Achilles tendonitis or rupture. The calf stretch shown in Photos 18 and 19 is also very important for women who wear heels all the time. Despite being an orthopaedic surgeon, I am one of these women. (I just can't help it.) For us, there is an added urgency of keeping our calves and Achilles flexible because when we wear heels, we walk around with our muscles in a shortened state. Our muscles can actually get so tight and short that we have pain even when walking in flat shoes.

You probably know this stretch already. Make sure that when you do it, you keep the leg straight to stretch your gastrocnemius and bent to stretch your soleus muscle. Both are important.

1. Stand with your feet shoulder length apart with your hands against a chair or a wall.

2. Keep your heels on the floor and your knees straight while leaning into the chair or wall (Photo 18). You will feel this stretch (in your gastrocnemius) down the back of your legs.

3. Hold for 30 seconds. Then bend your knees and continue leaning in (Photo 19). This stretches the deep soleus muscle.

4. Hold with bent knees for 30 seconds, then repeat with straight and bent knees four times.

This general stretching program hits all the major muscle groups in the body. As you make stretching a part of your everyday investment in health, you may find that you like doing some of these more than others and may even add things that are not listed here. That is great! It means that you are taking ownership of your body.

HOME**WORK**

I don't expect you to learn and implement these body-changing stretches all in one day. In order to learn them into your muscles, try doing the neck and upper body stretches three days this week and the low back and lower extremity stretches on the alternate three days. You can do them in your living room or take them on the road by downloading a podcast of some of my masters athletes taking you through them from my Web page at *www.fitnessafter40book.com*.

"The secret is this: there is no secret."

—Paraphrased from John L. Parker, Jr.,
Once a Runner (1978)

F.A.C.E.

Your Future Through A—
Aerobic Exercise

When it comes down to it, mastering fitness over 40 means maximizing performance by working hard enough to sweat. The secret is not a pill, a fountain, or a magic shot. Aging well is not a superficial process. Oh sure, looking good is as important to me as it is to you, but when I really feel the confidence that I am being "all that I can be" and strut down the street, it is because I look good and feel strong from the inside out.

I remember one day last January—the 14th, to be exact—when I was writing the proposal for this book. I felt so inspired by what I was writing that I just had to jump up and go for a run. It was one of those rare warm, sunny, beautiful winter days in New York's Central Park. There is a 1.7-mile loop with rolling hills in the south end of the park. As I neared the end of the first loop, I began to feel great and picked up my pace as I began the second round. It was one of those "out of body" days when I just marveled at how strong I felt. My arms were pumping, my legs were churning, and I was breathing deeply and sweating profusely. I knew that the hard work I had been putting in on the road, in spin class, and carrying weights around were clicking in that day! I felt so victorious . . . mastering my 40th year from the inside out. I remember specifically commenting on it to a friend, and I even wrote a note in my Day-Timer. Now, I am not an elite athlete. I am in the Fit category and just trying to maximize my performance and fitness like many of you. That takes work, but you can do it just like I did.

WHAT ABOUT YOU?

Do you think that just because you have celebrated life for a random number of years, you automatically must slow down or stop being active? Don't let anyone ever tell you this! The fact is that you are designed to move!

Do you remember Jabba the Hutt, that blob of meanness from the *Star Wars* film *The Return of the Jedi*? He had no legs, puny arms, a huge round belly, and a mouth that covered most of his face. All he was built for was lying around and being mean. Now there was a guy who was not designed to move. Unless you are one of his cousins, movement and activity are in your genes! We are built with strong extremities that respond to activity no matter what our chronologic age.

The key is understanding how you are different now from the way you were when you were 20 years old. Think about being "masterful" when you approach your next 30 or 40 years of activity.

BRING IN THE OXYGEN

In Chapter 4, we talked about staying flexible. The next step in F.A.C.E.-ing your future is getting your heart into the game through aerobic exercise, which means bringing oxygen into the picture. Just as your entire body can put on fat and become weak from disuse, so can your heart. If you don't challenge it, your heart literally becomes surrounded by a flabby envelope of fat and lub-dubs along like a floppy sac.

If you are just beginning to invest in your physical fitness, getting your heart into the game simply means getting off the couch and walking up the stairs instead of taking the escalator or elevator. The pounding you feel in your chest is your heart stepping up to duty. If you already exercise several times a week, the question becomes whether or not you are still challenging your heart or whether your usual exercise has become too easy.

WHAT IS AEROBIC EXERCISE?

Aerobic means "with oxygen," and aerobic exercise is exercise that involves oxygen. Let's take a step back and understand exactly what happens during aerobic exercise. When you increase your activity level and work your large muscle groups, your muscles require more fuel. Oxygen is the raw material or fuel used to make muscle food, a substance called ATP (adenosine triphosphate, or adenosine-5'-triphosphate). When you exercise, your muscles rapidly pull the oxygen out of your blood. Your brain senses the low oxygen levels and stimulates your body to respond very quickly by making you breathe more rapidly and more deeply. This maximizes the amount of oxygen in your lungs. Oxygen (which makes up 21 percent of the air we breathe) is then passed from your lungs into your blood, where it latches on to the hemoglobin molecules. It is then ready for transport to the muscle groups screaming for more fuel. This is where the heart comes in.

Blood that is now filled with oxygen (and thus appears red) moves from your lungs into the left side of your heart. Your heart is a muscle. Like any muscle, the stronger it is, the more efficient it is at doing its job, and the heart's job is to propel oxygen-rich blood from your lungs to all the tissues of your body.

The left side of your heart fills with blood and then, in a massive contraction, ejects the blood into the arteries that carry the blood to the tissues. (Remember: Arteries move blood *away* from the heart.) When oxygen is delivered to your muscle cells, it is exchanged for cell waste, such as carbon dioxide and lactic acid. The oxygen enters your cells and becomes part of a miraculous and complicated energy-generating system called the Krebs cycle (which, by the way, we all hated memorizing in medical school).

This highly efficient cycle churns out energy in the form of ATP (if oxygen were crude oil, then ATP is the unleaded gas that goes into our tanks). Your muscles use ATP for fuel. When your muscles are munching up the fuel faster than your heart can deliver oxygen—or the Krebs cycle can turn it into fuel—the cells switch to a faster but much less efficient anaerobic fuel system. This anaerobic (meaning without oxygen) system is 16 times less efficient than the Krebs cycle and produces the lactic acid that makes your muscles so sore after exercising.

The more fit your body is and efficient your heart becomes, the more work can be done with each given amount of oxygen.

In other words, if you were a car, the more efficient your heart engine, the better your miles per gallon or work per unit of oxygen would be.

WHY IS AEROBIC EXERCISE IMPORTANT TO YOU?

If I asked you, you could probably give me 10 or more really good reasons to do aerobic exercise. The problem is not that people don't know that aerobic exercise is the key to aging well. The problem is that only a third of us do 30 minutes of aerobic exercise a day! Where is the disconnect? We all have our reasons. I can assure you that I have heard every conceivable and some very creative reasons why my patients don't get off the couch 30 minutes a day and invest in aging well.

My friend, you cannot afford not to make a 30-minute daily investment in your health! In fact, I have an old quote from 1893 up on my website that reads: *"Those who think they have no time for bodily exercise will sooner or later have to find the time for illness."*

We have been talking for a long time about staying fit. Soon, I am going to summarize some important reasons for you to start or increase your aerobic exercise without one more minute of delay. I feel so strongly about the importance of your not delaying that I would not be offended at all if you put the book down right now and went for a brisk walk, run, row, or bike ride. All of these are fantastic ways to get your heart pumping and your muscles warm. You might also think about removing the pile of stuff cluttering your treadmill or elliptical machine and getting on.

There is a woman in one of my PRIMA START classes who puts on her workout clothes and attends our weekly sessions faithfully. When we meet, we have a 20–30 minute lecture about some aspect of fitness and then exercise as a group for the remainder of the time. After five weeks of meeting together, I discovered that when we transitioned from classroom to exercise, this faithful woman would slip away, get in her car, and drive home. She was hoping that she would become inspired enough to exercise by just sitting and listening. In my experience, becoming inspired to exercise does not come from sitting on the couch or in classroom and watching and listening. Real inspiration comes when you get out on the road and sweat. When the program coordinators and I discovered that this woman was merely watching and not investing in herself, we exercised with her for the next couple of sessions. It was hard for her since she had not challenged herself for years. But at the end of the workouts, she was so proud of her accomplishment. In the same way, I want you to begin exercising while you read this book. Start now and add to your regimen as you read on.

The Reasons for Exercising: What You Already Know

- *Cardiovascular*. Multiple studies have proved that physically fit people have a lower death rate than sedentary people. Exercise increases the amount of blood your heart ejects with each beat and the total volume of blood leaving the heart. In turn, this increases the amount and efficiency of oxygen reaching your muscles and organs. Exercise also lowers the heart muscle's demand for oxygen because it uses the oxygen fuel more efficiently.

- *Diabetes*. Exercise improves the body's response to insulin and lowers the risk of developing diabetes by 30–40 percent. Exercise can also decrease a diabetic's risk of dying of heart disease by 40–50 percent.

- *Blood pressure*. Many studies have shown that regular exercise lowers your blood pressure, and thus the work your heart has to do. This effect is independent of a person's age or body mass index or the presence of diabetes.

- *Cholesterol*. Exercise increases the level of "good cholesterol" (HDL) in your blood, which acts like Drano® to clean out your blood vessels. At the same time, exercise lowers the level of "bad cholesterol" (LDL) and triglycerides (which are dangerous fats) and prevents the bad stuff from sticking to the sides of your blood vessels. Exercise also enhances the beneficial effect of a low-fat diet.

- *SeDS (Sedentary Death Syndrome)*. Although it may sound like a joke, SeDS is no laughing matter. The ill effects of more than 35 chronic diseases can be directly decreased by 30 minutes of exercise a day.

The Reasons for Exercising: Amazing Things You May Not Know

- *Brain function*. Exercise makes a type of Miracle-Gro for the brain—really! When exercising, your brain makes a substance called brain-derived neurotrophic factor, which is a type of brain food. Studies have found that active people are more likely to be better adjusted and perform better on tests of cognitive function. And scientists believe this exercise-induced "brain food" is the reason.

- *Mood*. After a stressful day, exercise can calm and improve your mood. According to researchers at the University of Missouri, thirty minutes of moderate-to-intense aerobic exercise can leave you still feeling on top of the world ninety minutes later. This is because exercise causes the brain to release endorphins, which are natural mood elevators. It's like popping an antidepressant pill but with exercise. People who exercise are 1.5 times less likely to be depressed; they also have higher self-confidence and higher self-esteem than people who do not exercise. This is true for both chronic exercisers and adult onset exercisers. This effect holds true as long as you are exercising. If you stop exercising, the mood benefits fade with your general fitness. Regular exercise also improves self-confidence and self-esteem while decreasing the cardiac and hormonal responses to mental stress, such as a racing heart, abundant sweating, and feeling on edge.

- *Erectile dysfunction*. For some of the same reasons exercise is good for your heart, exercise is great for sexual function. Physiologically, erection is all about healthy blood flow, and men who exercise have been found to have 41 percent less erectile dysfunction than those who sit on the couch.

- *Immune function and sickness*. Both athlete surveys and randomized studies (done on all sorts of people) have shown that people who do moderate exercise on a near daily basis experience fewer sick days. Exercisers report taking about half the number of sick days as their sedentary peers and having 23 percent fewer upper respiratory tract infections.

- *Cancer prevention*. Exercise can decrease the risk of breast cancer by up to 60 percent by lowering levels of two of the ovarian hormones linked to breast cancer, estradiol and progesterone. Exercise also can decrease the risk of colorectal cancer by 40 percent and decrease the risk of dying from prostate cancer by 50 percent. If you have or have had cancer, exercise can be of great physical and mental benefit.

HOW DO I START?

If you are just beginning to exercise, read the seven questions listed below. This is a simple checklist, designed by the Canadian Society for Exercise Physiology, to determine whether or not you

THE EXERCISE-CANCER CONNECTION

There are many physical and mental benefits that exercise exerts on cancer, especially breast and prostate cancer. If you have or have had breast cancer, research published in 2005 suggests that a few hours of walking or other exercise each week may help you live longer. In a Harvard University study of nearly 3,000 women, those who exercised the equivalent of walking about one hour a week at a pace of two to three miles per hour had a lower risk of dying from breast cancer than women who got less than an hour's worth of physical activity each week. Women who did a little more than that—the equivalent of walking about three to five hours per week at the same pace—had the lowest risk of dying. Women who got more exercise than that also had a lower risk of dying, but not as low as women in the middle group.[1] In short, doing three to five hours of physical activity is better than straining to do more.

This finding could give you another way to boost your odds of beating breast cancer. "Women with breast cancer have little to lose and much to gain from exercise," said the study's lead author, Michelle Holmes, MD, DrPH, of Harvard Medical School and Brigham and Women's Hospital in Boston. "We already know that [breast cancer patients who exercise] have better mood, better body image, and better self-esteem. We know it [exercise] fights other diseases that women with breast cancer can also get, like heart disease and diabetes. And it may also help these women avoid dying from breast cancer."[2]

The same benefits from exercise hold true for men with prostate cancer. Decreased physical activity, which may be the result of the cancer itself or the treatment for it, can lead to tiredness and lack of energy. Results of the Health Professional Follow-up Study of 47,000 men over a 14-year period, published in the *Annals of Internal Medicine* in 2005, showed that men over age 65 who engaged in at least three hours of vigorous physical activity (such as running, biking, or swimming) per week had a nearly 70 percent lower risk of being diagnosed with advanced prostate cancer or dying from the disease. Researchers say more study is needed to understand how exercise affects prostate cancer risk in men of all ages, but these findings show that vigorous exercise may slow the progression of prostate cancer in older men.

In another finding, by researchers at UCLA's Jonsson Cancer Center and Department of Physiological Science, a low-fat, high-fiber diet and regular exercise reportedly slowed prostate cancer cell growth by up to 30 percent. Study participants walked at 70 to 85 percent of their maximum heart rate four to five times per week for 30 to 60 minutes, and once or twice a week at a slower pace for 40 to 60 minutes. "This is the first study to directly measure the effects of diet and exercise on inhibiting prostate cancer cell growth," said Dr. William Aronson, senior author of the study. "We used a new method, developed by our research team, to evaluate how effectively these lifestyle changes might help slow the growth of prostate cancer cells, and we are extremely encouraged by the results."[3]

need to check with your doctor to receive medical clearance to exercise. When in doubt, however, always see your doctor.

1. Has your doctor ever said that you have a heart condition and that you should do only physical activity recommended by a doctor?
2. Do you feel pain in your chest when you do physical exercise?
3. In the past month, have you had chest pain when you were not doing exercise?

4. Do you lose your balance because of dizziness, or do you ever lose consciousness?

5. Do you have a bone or joint problem that could be made worse by a change in your physical activity?

6. Is your doctor currently prescribing drugs for your blood pressure or heart condition?

7. Do you know of any other reason why you should not do physical activity?

If you answered *no* to all seven questions, you can be reasonably sure that you can start becoming more physically active if you start slowly and build up gradually. You could also participate in a community fitness appraisal to determine your basic fitness level. Many community health centers, YMCAs, or gyms bring in medical personnel to perform these health overviews. Be aware that if you answered *no* to all of the questions because you have not been to the doctor in years, then now is the time to get checked out.

If you answered *yes* to one or more of the above questions, you should talk to your doctor by phone or in person before starting to increase your activity. You may still be able to do any activity you want by starting slowly and increasing gradually. However, your doctor will have the opportunity to discuss the activities you'd like to participate in. In addition, by the American Heart Association recommends that anyone with known heart disease see his doctor prior to beginning an exercise program.

When you visit your doctor, she will interview you and review the cardiovascular risk factors listed on page 76. An electrocardiogram (EKG) will be done to look at your heart function. If you have a moderate- to high-risk profile for heart disease,

CARDIOVASCULAR RISK FACTORS

Moderate cardiac risk is defined as men 40–45 years old or women 50–55 years old with one of more of the following:

- Total cholesterol of more than 200 mg/dL

- LDL (low density lipoprotein—the bad cholesterol) of more than 130 mg/dL

- HDL (high density lipoprotein—the good cholesterol) of less than 35 mg/dL

- High blood pressure of more than 140/90 mm Hg

- Current or recent cigarette smoking

- Diabetes or fasting blood sugar of less than 126 mg/dL

- A history of sudden cardiac death in a member of your immediate family who was less than 60 years old

have known cardiovascular disease, or are older than 65 with no risk factors, your doctor may also want to perform an exercise stress test.

HOW DO I KNOW I AM EXERCISING ENOUGH?

How do we know when we are exercising enough (aerobically with oxygen) and not too much (anaerobically without oxygen)? For an effective workout, you need to exercise within your target heart rate and stay there for 20 minutes or more. Raising your heart rate and keeping it up burns fat, increases your cardiovascular fitness, and actually keeps the heart muscle itself healthy.

You can calculate your target heart rate by following these three steps:

1. Subtract your age from 220. This is your maximum heart rate (MaxHR).
2. Multiple your MaxHR by 0.85. This is your maximum target rate.
3. Multiple your MaxHR by 0.50. This is your minimum target rate.

If you are 50 years old, your MaxHR is 220 -50, or 170 beats per minute. Multiplying 170 by 0.85 gives you a maximum target rate of 144. Multiplying 170 by 0.50 gives you a minimum target rate of 85. Thus, your target heart range is 85 to 144.

You can use your target heart rate to help achieve your goals. Working out at 60–70 percent of MaxHR is best for weight management and a fit appearance; 70–80 percent puts you in the heart-healthy aerobic zone; and 80–100 percent gives you the competitive edge for peak performance.

During your workouts, periodically check your heart rate. If you have a heart rate monitor (a device worn on your chest and wrist that can detect and track your heart rate while you are being active), you can set the alarm limits around your target heart range.

If you do not have a monitor, you can get a rough estimate of your heart rate by counting your pulse for six seconds and adding a zero. You can check your pulse by placing your index and middle fingers lightly on your radial pulse. This is the pulse on the thumb side of your wrist. Press lightly because pressing too heavily will cut off the flow of blood through the vessel, and you will be unable to count. You can also place your fingers lightly on either side of your windpipe (the hard tube you feel in the very center of your throat) to feel your carotid pulse. Do not press too hard or massage this area since this can affect your heart rate. Practice taking your pulse before you start to exercise so you know what you are feeling for before you exercise. If your heart rate is too slow, pick up your pace; if it is too high, then slow down a bit.

If you continually exercise above your target range, your heart may not be able to keep up with your oxygen demand, and you will switch from the efficient aerobic form of exercise to the inefficient anaerobic form. The anaerobic form produces lactic acid as a byproduct and causes muscle soreness.

As you get into shape, your target heart rate will not change. However, the work that you have to do to get your heart into that range will change. The better shape you are in, the more efficient your heart is and the lower your resting heart rate will become. You will have to put forth more effort to raise your heart rate. For instance, when you first step away from the couch, it may take only a moderately paced walk to get your heart into the 60–70 percent of MaxHR zone. As you become more fit, however, you may need to walk briskly or even jog to get your heart rate up. Your heart has become more efficient and does more work with each stroke.

Here is an example of how to use workout time and target heart rate together. Let's say you are running on a track for 30 minutes. When you begin to exercise, you may be able to run only four laps and keep your heart in the target range. As you become more fit, however, you may be able increase your speed and cover five laps or eventually six laps in the same time period without working outside your target heart range. By now, you will be feeling a noticeable change in your daily stamina, state of mind, and energy level. As you get in better shape, you can increase the intensity or the duration of your workout. You will find that as you increase the duration of your aerobic activity, your heart rate may go up toward the end. This is the effect of fatigue. When your heart rate remains in the target zone until the end of your workout, then it is time to increase the amount of workout time or intensity again.

For those of you already working out, you can increase your performance by increasing the intensity of your workout from 60–70 percent to 70–80 percent of MaxHR. (You can calculate this as explained above.) Once you are able to move through your workout comfortably at this intensity, you can continue improving by adding time or distance. For instance, you can increase your aerobic period from 30 to 45 minutes or increase the intensity of your 30-minute workout to 70–80 percent of MaxHR. If long distance running (marathon or a half-marathon) is your goal, you should build your endurance base in the 60–70 percent MaxHR zone. This means that while your shorter midweek runs can be 70–80 percent intense, those long weekend runs should slow down to 60–70 percent intensity.

A fun way to improve your fitness is to do fartlek runs. *Fartlek* is a Swedish word that means "speed play." This method of increasing your workout intensity alternates running at an easy pace with running at your maximum heart rate. Fartleks allow you to work out without getting tired because as soon as you reach the upper limit of your MaxHR, you immediately slow down to walk or jog until your heart rate recovers. An example of a fartlek would be starting with a one-mile jog at 60–70 percent effort. When you reach this point, you pick up your speed and run faster or even sprint until your heart reaches 85 percent of your MaxHR, and then you immediately slow down again until your heart rate returns to 60–70 percent. You then speed up again. You keep alternating slow/fast for a set period of time (20 or 30 minutes, for example) and increase the intensity of the workout by increasing the duration. This is a great way to work from walking to running. You can find other examples of how to apply the fartlek technique to your workouts at *www.fitnessafter40book.com*.

Hal Higdon is a runner and writer who is well known for his contributions to *Runner's World* magazine. When I ramp up for races, I always use his workout schedules. On his website (*www.halhigdon.com*), he has created different workout patterns, and you choose one according to whether you want to work out at a novice, intermediate, or advanced level. He suggests ways to improve by adding hills, tempo runs (practice runs at race pace), and intervals to the speed play. Many other online coaches suggest specific regimens for race preparation. I find Higdon's to be very useful—and free.

To begin your own exercise program, choose the aerobic activity you are going to start doing, such as walking, hiking, running, jogging, aerobic dance, rope skipping, stairs, skating, cycling, skiing, aerobics classes, rowing, swimming, and endurance sports. Keep track of what your heart is doing. I find that the easiest way to track what my heart is doing and be precise about my workouts is to wear a heart rate monitor.

KEEP IT SIMPLE

When you are getting started, it is important to keep it simple. Do not make an elaborate plan with multilevel goals. Go for a walk, run, swim, or row—anything that is logistically practical for you. Remember that just making the decision to exercise does not erase years of sedentary buildup, so don't try to make it up all at once. Many people start with walking first. It is simple and logistically practical since you can just open the front door and start, and let's face it, there is no new skill to learn.

In addition to being simple, you also need to be very specific when you are planning your upcoming launch into activity. Know the activity and the day and time you will participate in it, as well as what you hope to accomplish before you begin. Write it down in your calendar or set an alarm on your phone.

Being strategic in your planning is very important. You strategically plan every day in business, your finances, and your social activities. Why not apply the same discipline that works in other parts of your life to caring for your body? A daily strategic plan might read:

Saturday at 3:30 P.M.: Walk in North Park for 35 minutes with my heart rate at 65 percent maximum. Make a plan for each day of the week even if the plan for Sunday says: *Rest and restore all day*. In Chapter 14, you will find suggestions on how to make a six-week plan. Each of the weeks should have a strategic plan where you reward yourself.

Place your workout plan prominently in your life, posting it on your refrigerator, bathroom mirror, computer calendar, and so on.

GET WARMED UP

You must warm up before taking off on your exercise adventure. This can take the form of an easy walk or a slow jog before a run, or a few slow pool laps before you turn up the speed. Dynamic warm-ups—warm-ups where you are moving and stretching instead of just standing in one place—are fun and get the heart pumping and the muscles filled with blood. The following warm-up exercises can easily be performed before any kind of exercise.

Photo 20   Photo 21

Hip circles

Hip circles, shown in Photos 20 and 21, warm up the large muscles in the front and back of your midsection and buttocks.

1. Begin with your hands on your hips and your feet together.
2. Bend one leg up in front of the body at the hip (Photo 20) and rotate it up to the side (Photo 21), then lower it.
3. Reverse the movement by bending the leg up at the hip to the side and rotating it forward before lowering it.
4. Repeat this ten times.
5. Perform on the opposite leg.

Photo 22   Photo 23

Lunge

This lunge, shown in Photos 22 and 23, not only warms up your hips and buttocks but also stretches your hips flexor muscles.

1. Stand with your feet together.
2. Hug one of your knees to your chest (Photo 22) and then release your leg.
3. Lunge onto that knee while trying to keep your knee above your ankle and not in front of it (Photo 23).
4. Bring your back leg forward until you are standing again.
5. Repeat ten times, and progress forward.
6. Perform with the opposite leg.

Inchworm

The inchworm—shown in Photos 24, 25, and 26—is harder than it looks. The inchworm warms up your legs while giving a good stretch to the hamstrings and calf muscles that run down the backs of your legs.

1. Begin in a push-up position (Photo 24).
2. Slowly walk your legs toward your hands (Photo 25). Heels may be off the floor.

Photo 24

Photo 25 (feet walk forward)

Photo 26 (hands walk forward)

3. Continue walking forward until the pull in the back of your legs is uncomfortable.

4. At this point, slowly walk your arms forward with your feet still, until you are back in the push-up position (Photo 26).

5. Repeat this inching along five to ten times.

Toe and Heel Walks

Walking on your toes gives your calves, in the back of your lower legs, a good warm-up. Walking on your heels warms up the front portion of your legs as well as warming up your ankles. If your legs start to ache while doing either of these walks, you should stop.

1. Walk on your toes with your toes pointed straight ahead for about 20 meters, getting as high up on your toes as you possibly can. Your legs should be relatively straight as you do this, and you should—at least initially—take fairly small steps.

2. Switch to walking on your toes with your feet rotated out for 20 meters.

3. Do the same with your toes pointed in for 20 meters.

4. Repeat this while walking on your heels.

Skip

Did you think skipping was just for kids? It's not, and it's a good way for you to warm up.

1. Skip for 20 meters, landing in the mid-foot area with each contact with the ground, and with toes pointed straight ahead.

2. Try skipping by flexing your knees up high and taking longer than normal strides.

Skipping can also be used to vary your runs. Sometimes when I am tired and bored during a marathon, I switch to skipping for a few hundred meters to break it up a bit.

Rhythm Bounding

Bounding is just what it sounds like. You spring up into the air with each step you take. It looks like you are jogging with high knees in slow motion.

1. On a springy surface such as a rubber track or grass field, jog with short springy steps while landing on the mid-foot area, not on your toes.
2. Spring upward once after each impact. This warms up your ankles and legs by making them act like coiled springs. You move forward and upward with each step.

A great way to get the most out of your dynamic warm-up is to jog/walk for 20–30 yards between each exercise set.

TAKE 10,000 STEPS

One easy way to increase the overall activity in your life is to use the 10,000 step method. In this method, which originated in Japan, you monitor the activity you do during a day, making you conscious of the number of steps you take. Then you try to increase your activity and number of steps. You need a pedometer, which you can buy in most sporting goods stores; some are even given away at workplaces.

Wear the pedometer when you go out the door in the morning, and keep it on as you do your usual activities. When you go to bed at night, take it off and record the number of steps you took. Do this for a week. I think you will be surprised to learn how much or how little you actually travel in one day using your own two feet.

A sedentary person usually covers only 1,000 to 3,000 steps per day between his house, car, workplace, errands, and back. This is not far enough to cause meaningful changes in your fitness level. Using a pedometer and counting your steps is a good way to get yourself off the couch and become more aware of the activity you actually do each day. Once you are off the couch, you can increase your activity each day by increasing the number of steps you take.

But what is the big deal with taking a lot of steps, you ask? Many of us spend our work day sitting at a sedentary job. Research has shown that people who work in a seated position for most of the day have a higher risk of dying from cardiac disease than people in the same industry who have more active jobs: Bus drivers are more at risk than conductors, for example, and postal workers are more at risk than the people who carry and deliver the mail. In addition, executives who rest all weekend are more at risk than executives who participate in vigorous exercise on weekends. The findings applied whether or not the people had other risk factors—high blood pressure, smoking, obesity, or family history. What this means is that even if you have one of the four other major causes of cardiac disease, activity can still decrease your risk!

To become more fit and control chronic disease, we need to take 10,000 steps a day. If the average person has a stride length of 2.5 feet, this means that it takes about 2,000 steps to cover a mile; 10,000 steps a day would then be about five miles of activity. This can include your 30 minutes of aerobic activity and usually must in order to get that many steps in.

I found this was true for me. When I lived in New York and didn't have a car, I would walk to work, the store, the gym, restaurants . . . everywhere I needed to go. But I found that unless I actually went for a run, I did not accumulate 10,000 steps. I lived a mile from Central Park and would walk there, run three miles, and walk back and still have only about 6,500 steps on my pedometer. That meant I needed my usual daily walking plus a workout to get enough activity.

If you are going to use a pedometer and count your steps, don't get discouraged. Ten thousand steps is a nice round number to aim for, but if your goal is only to prevent weight gain, you may not need to log that many steps. You can build up gradually and be more active on some days than on others. What is important is that you are off the couch!

HOW TO START YOUR WORKOUT

When you begin your workout, you may want to use time as the measure of your work initially instead of distance. For instance, if you are going to start your workout by walking, begin at a comfortable pace for 10 minutes to warm up. Then stop and do the leg stretching exercises you learned in Chapter 4. Alternatively, you can do the dynamic warm-up. When you are warmed-up, begin exercising again at a pace that elevates your heart rate to within your target range. This means that unless you have a heart rate monitor, you may have to stop momentarily to take your pulse, but that's okay. If you are working hard enough, you should recognize your aerobic system kicking in. Your breathing will be getting quicker and deeper and you may feel your heart beating faster in your chest. Continue exercising for at least 20 minutes. It's okay if you need to slow down or even stop to rest initially.

Over the next several weeks, you will build up to a continuous 20 minutes of exercise. When you are able to do this, increase your workout by two to five minutes each week until you are able to do 30 continuous minutes within your target heart rate zone. I encourage you to use the principles discussed in this chapter for increasing your activity level and volume.

Think about how you would like to use your workout time, and make a plan that will work for you. This way, the plan belongs to you and you are more likely to adhere to it. If, however, you would like to use a simple plan that works with my patients, you can follow along beginning in Chapter 14.

WHY ARE YOU EXERCISING?

You need to answer an important question about your activity. Why are you exercising? What is the point of your activity? Is it to get better and get in shape, or just continue to do what comes easily to you? If the point is to improve, then challenge yourself and take it up to the next level.

I was having a discussion with *New York Times* journalist Gina Kolata about why men seem more likely to challenge themselves to the next level of fitness than women (a topic for another time). As we were talking, she mentioned an insightful comment her 17-year-old son had made to her: "Mom, why are you running anyway?" He did not mean that she should list the 30 good reasons to get and stay in shape. Instead, he wanted to know why, after all this time, she was still jogging along at pace that now felt like a walk in the park.

WHAT 15 MINUTES CAN DO FOR YOU

Before you start to say, "I just don't have time," look around. I know you can find 15 minutes once, twice, three times a day. Look at what you can accomplish in 15 minutes:

Activity	Calories Burned
Stair climbing	150
Running	150
Jumping rope	150
Shoveling snow	120
Playing football	120
Playing tennis	100
Walking	75
Bicycling	75
Swimming	75
Washing floors	70
Dancing	70
Light housework	60–70
Desk work	30
Sleeping	18
Watching TV	18

I can identify with this question, too. For years, I ran at the same pace because it was easy. Not until I worked out more smartly and intensely did I drop my time per mile.

If you are just getting off the couch, the challenge is to get moving. But if you are in the Fit category, you need to take a look at what you are doing and whether or not it has become too easy for you.

HOME**WORK**

1. Practice counting your heart rate.

2. Calculate your maximum heart rate and your 60–70 percent and 70–80 percent heart rate ranges.

3. Take 10 minutes to warm up slowly.

4. If you are just beginning to get active, go for a 20-minute walk and get your heart rate up to 60–70 percent and see what it feels like.

5. If you are already fit, mix up your workout with a fun fartlek. Make sure you warm up first!

NOTES

1. Holmes, Michelle D. et al., "Physical Activity and Survival After Breast Cancer Diagnosis," *Journal of the American Medical Association* 293(20): 2479–2486 (2005).

2. American Cancer Society, "Exercise Can Improve Breast Cancer Survival," www.cancer.org/docroot/NWS/content/NWS_1_1x_ Exercise_Can_Improve_Breast_Cancer_Survival.asp.

3. UniSci, "Diet, Exercise Slow Prostate Cancer As Much As 30%," www.unisci.com/stories/20013/0911013.htm.

"There is a difference between interest and commitment. When you're interested in doing something, you do it only when circumstances permit. When you're committed to something, you accept no excuses, only results."

—Motivational speaker and writer Art Turock

6

F.A.C.E.

Your Future by C—Carrying a Load

What is "carrying a load?" It simply means resistance training or weight lifting. Resistance training is important because of its role in building and maintaining muscle.

I am always shocked when I see the X-rays of one of my patient's legs. X-rays are for looking at the bones, but we can see shadows of the soft tissues around the bones. Sometimes there is only a thin layer of muscle surrounding the bone and a thick layer of fat under the skin. This can be the case for both heavy people and thin people if they are not strong. We need strong, thick muscles to do everything from getting out of a chair, to climbing a flight of stairs, to preventing falls, as well as to jog around the block. Just because a person looks in the mirror and sees a thick thigh does not mean that he has enough muscle to support his bones and joints. On the other hand, thin does not mean fit. Thin can mean that there is not enough muscle.

With muscle, you truly will lose it if you don't use it. Have you ever had your arm or leg in a cast? Do you remember how tight the cast was against your skin when the doctor put it on? Perhaps it even felt confining and uncomfortable. Within a week or so, the cast became looser, and you could see clear space between it and your skin. This was the result of disuse atrophy of the muscle. Essentially, this is what happens to your entire body if you don't actively use your muscles.

Once your muscle is lost, do you weigh less? No. The five pounds of muscle we lose is typically replaced with five pounds of fat. This fat makes us bigger all around because a pound of fat takes up 18 percent more room on our frame than a pound of muscle.

Pushing and pulling weight around is vital for fitness after 40. If aging progresses unchecked, we lose 10 percent of our muscle mass between the ages of 25 and 50, and 45 percent more between ages 50 and 80. This loss of lean muscle mass (or sarcopenia) leaves us vulnerable to falls, poor bone health, and an inability to do the things we want to do physically each day. To stave off muscle decline, you must carry a load. There are also many other benefits to carrying a load as part of your exercise regimen. Not only does it make you look great but it keeps your bones strong, lowers your blood pressure, and may reduce the risk of stroke. In addition, it burns more calories during activities of daily living than fat. If you build up your muscles so that a great percentage of your body is muscle rather than fat, you will use more calories for simply living than you did when you had less muscle and more fat. Maintaining and building muscle is good for your metabolism, makes you strong, prevents falling, prevents injury, and lifts your mood. Because loss of muscle increases markedly after age 50, lifting weights after 50 is critical.

There are countless articles in the medical and exercise physiology literature that document the fact that muscle disuse atrophy is reversible in both mature athletes and aging couch potatoes. In as little as eight to12 weeks, resistance training can produce marked improvements in strength and endurance.

An old study from 1993 looked at two groups of masters athletes. One group ran 30 minutes three times per week, while the other group ran 15 minutes three times per week and carried a load with all their major muscle groups for the remaining 15 minutes. At the end of four months, bone density and lean muscle mass increased significantly in the group that did resistance work along with running, while bone density and lean muscle mass did not increase in the group that only did running.

With a low repetition/high weight regimen, both masters athletes and active agers can show similar or greater strength gains compared with younger people. A two- to three-fold increase in muscle strength can be accomplished in a relatively short period of time (12 weeks) with moderately intense workouts. In addition, heavy resistance training improves the amount of protein your body retains no matter how much you eat. With weight lifting, even people eating lower protein diets can build muscle because they retain more of what they eat.

Many studies document much greater muscle mass, architecture, and functional strength in strength-trained masters athletes than their sedentary peers. It is not only the quantity of muscle that improves but the muscle is actually better in quality. Both the amount and quality of muscle is dependent on the intensity of the exercise performed. This means that lifting heavier weights is better than lifting light weights.

Strength training has other benefits as well. It is an important part of weight management as we age. It is associated with increased energy requirements for rest, which means that you simply use more energy just to live if you have more muscle. How many more calories? Research in the Netherlands documented a nine percent greater calorie burn with resistance training. Even without diet changes, this will translate into lost pounds. A big bonus of strength training is also more effective insulin sensitivity for people with diabetes. The more muscle you have, the better your body responds to the insulin you take or make by lowering your blood sugar. A true weekly weight program can decrease insulin levels by 25 percent after a high-carbohydrate meal. Finally, carrying a load not only strengthens bone and increases muscle mass and strength, but the combination of these factors decreases the incidence of falls and thus osteoporotic fractures (fractures that occur because of weak bone).

Lifting weights may evoke images of big sweaty guys hoisting iron plates onto sagging metal crossbars and grunting out the effort as they push the weight around. Carrying a load does not, however, have to be a burden, and you do not have to do endless repetitions of heavy weights to receive a benefit. In fact, it is not necessary to haul steel around at all. One of the best "loads" to carry is your own body weight.

HOW TO CARRY A LOAD

When carrying a load, start by working the large muscle groups first and then progress to the smaller ones. You can begin with your arms or legs. With the legs, begin with your buttocks or quadriceps before moving down the leg to the smaller calf muscles. With the arms, begin with the pectoralis (chest), biceps, triceps, etc., before moving to the smaller rotator cuff muscles in the upper arm. This way, you get the most demanding work out of the way when you are not so tired. How fast you move through the lift is also important. Lifting should be slow and controlled, never jerking.

There are a lot of different ways to carry a load. It is not necessary to have access to a weight machine. Free weights—such as dumbbells, exercise bands, and your own body—are all excellent weights to carry. (More on exercise bands, which look like heavy-duty rubber bands, in a few paragraphs.) Some strength coaches actually prefer free weights and exercise bands over stationary machines because they require the lifter to engage the pathways between your brain and muscles to control and balance the weights. Don't forget: In this age of high-tech gym equipment, it can be highly effective to lift just your own upper body weight with push-ups and chin-ups and your lower body weight with short arc squats. Short arc squats are described later in this chapter.

Research has shown that you can receive 60 percent of the total benefit from resistance training by doing one set of eight to ten repetitions per muscle group two to three times per week, and more than 80 percent of the benefit by doing two sets. Each repetition should be between 60 and 85 percent of the maximum weight you are able to lift one time, or your one-rep maximum.

To find your one-rep max, if you are using a weight machine, simply keep increasing the weight until you can do only one repetition of the load. Make sure you are not jerking the weight since you could hurt yourself. If you are using dumbbells, find the maximum you can lift the same way. If you are using exercise bands, progress up in thickness until you are using the one that is hardest for you to stretch. (Exercise bands come in different colors to indicate different strengths. Generally, they progress from yellow, which is the lightest, to red, green, blue, gray, and black, which is the heaviest.)

Once you determine your maximum weight for a muscle group, calculate what 70 to 80 percent of that is. This will be your workout weight. For instance, I can curl 20 pounds with my left (nondominant) bicep one time. Eighty percent of that is 16 pounds. I therefore work out with a 15-pound dumbbell (there is no 16-pound dumbbell), and I do one set of ten repetitions. Remember that with one set, you get 60 percent of the benefit, and with two sets, you get more than 80 percent. I have settled on one set because of time constraints; one set is sufficient to keep my arms strong and fit.

Lifting more than 85 percent of your maximum can increase your risk of injury, while lifting less than 60 percent is not effective. This means that the total number of reps can be low, but the weight should be intense. Each repetition should be taken through a full range of motion in a slow, controlled motion. You should take twice as long to lower the weight as you do to lift it. For instance, you can do biceps curls with either a free weight or tubing. (Resistance tubes are like large rubber bands that you pull. Depending on their size, they offer different degrees of resistance and therefore the amount of work your muscles do. They come in a variety of colors, with each color representing a different resistance strength. You should start with a color that you have to work to pull but that is not so resistant that it hurts or that you cannot complete a set of 10.) When you do biceps curls, if you lift the weight by bending your elbow for two seconds, then you should take four seconds to extend your elbow and lower the weight. Do not jerk the weight up. Jerking the weight up is a good way to tear your musculotendonous junction (the connection between your muscles and your tendons).

When you have been using one weight level for a while, lifting may become easy. This is called adaptation. To continue getting stronger, you must increase the weight you are lifting. The time to increase the weight is when you can easily lift your current weight 12 times. You can then progress your weight by 5 percent and decrease your repetitions to eight.

Remember that when you are standing in front of the mirror watching your muscles flex and bulge, you will not see them getting bigger. During active weight lifting, you are actually creating tiny microtears in the muscle substance. It is during your rest periods every other day between workouts that your muscles repair and rebuild to increase in size and strength.

MUSCLE GROUPS TO COVER IN YOUR WEIGHT TRAINING

Upper Extremities

- *Latissimus dorsi.* The big V-shaped back muscles.

- *Rotator cuff.* Four small muscles that provide shoulder stability by keeping the arm bone (the humerus) centered in the socket. The rotator cuff is the key to shoulder health.

- *Biceps.* The "guns" in the front of your upper arm.

- *Triceps.* Gun balancers in the back of your upper arm.

- *Deltoid muscles.* The shoulder caps.

- *Wrist extensors.* Muscles in the back of the lower arm.

- *Wrist flexors.* Muscles in the front of the lower arm.

The Core

- *The core.* The weight belt of muscles around your front that are the key to the health of your back.

Lower Extremities

- *Buttocks.*

- *Hip flexors.* The muscles that flex your hip up.

- *Quadriceps.* Four large muscles in the front of the thighs that are the key to healthy knees.

- *Hamstrings.* Muscles in the back of the thighs that flex your knees back.

- *Anterior tibialis.* A muscle in the front of the shin.

- *Gastrocnemius.* A muscle in the calves.

FITNESS TO GO

There are four key areas that I want you to know by heart. I call them my "Fitness to Go" workout. These areas represent the four most common areas of complaint that weekend warriors and active agers bring into my office to investigate. They are:

1. Leg and ankle tendonitis
2. Knee pain
3. Low back pain
4. Shoulder pain

With my Fitness to Go exercises, you can prevent problems in these key areas.

The beauty of the simple set of resistance exercises that follow is that they are portable. You don't need special machines to do them, and you can take them with you when you travel for business or pleasure. You can hang exercise bands from your office door and get in a few exercise sets between clients, or keep the bands around the house and work in a set whenever you have a free minute. You can even stick the bands in your purse and work out on the go!

Fitness to Go covers the key focus areas for preventing and minimizing the deleterious effects of injury. These exercises strengthen the muscle groups most susceptible to injury preemptively and prepare you for sports battle.

You may have performed many of the weight-lifting maneuvers in the following pages at some point in your life. If you don't remember them or never did them before, you can go to my website at *www.fitnessafter40book.com* and download a podcast of some of my masters patients taking you through a routine. This is an easy way for you to take all this information on the road or to the gym with you.

FITNESS TO GO: YOUR BACK

The key to your back is your front. The muscles of the lower back are actually smaller than the muscles of the abdomen and sides. The large rectus muscles in the front and the oblique muscles on your sides—also known as your core—stabilize your back and pelvis and, if strong, act to prevent pain. The most important way to prevent low back pain and the misery it causes is to concentrate on your core muscles. Core strength is also vital for all sports from running (runners notoriously have weak core strength) to golf (how do you think Tiger Woods drives the ball so far?). No matter what your sport, you have a weak core only because you do not specifically pay attention to it.

So what is your core? Your core is the "belt" of muscles that wraps around your midsection. It consists of the rectus muscles that give you the "six-pack" look of your stomach. More importantly, these oblique or diagonal muscles, which wrap around the sides of your body from back to front, form a natural weight belt. Place you hands just above your hips and tighten the muscles under your palms. (You can do this not by sucking in your stomach but by pushing down on the pelvis with your muscles. Although indelicate, it is almost like pushing down to have a bowel movement.) Engaging this natural weight belt is called "bracing." Once you start bracing these muscles frequently, you will notice them getting tight. If you can't feel them getting tight now, it does not mean they are not there; they just have not been engaged in a long time. Your goal is to keep these muscles working throughout the day even when you are not exercising.

You should perform the following core exercises at least three days a week. Do them while relaxing after work. If you can only do one of the exercises, choose the plank.

Leg Abduction

Photo 27 shows the leg abduction.

Photo 27

1. While lying on your side, brace your abdominal muscles.

2. Bend your lower leg forward at the hip and support your trunk with your upper arm (as shown in Photo 27).

3. Raise your upper leg off the floor and behind your body. Do not let your trunk sag backward.

4. Concentrate on keeping your core engaged, and feel this in your buttocks.

5. Repeat the leg lift ten times, then switch to the other side.

Leg Adduction

Photo 28 shows the leg adduction.

Photo 28

1. While lying on your side, brace your abdomen.

2. Bend your top knee and place your top foot in front of your bottom knee.

3. Raise your lower leg off the floor (as shown in Photo 28). Do not let your trunk bend backward.

4. Concentrate on keeping your core engaged, and feel this on the inside of your lower leg.

5. Repeat the leg lift ten times, then switch to the other side.

You can combine the leg abduction and leg adduction exercises. While lying on the first side, do the leg abduction. Then, before switching to the other side and without resting, do the leg adduction. You can then switch to the other side and begin the leg abduction.

Dying Bug

Photos 29 and 30 shows the dying bug.

Photo 29

Photo 30

1. While lying on your back, raise one arm over your head and bend the opposite knee to 90 degrees.
2. Brace your core muscles.

3. Without swaying your back, raise the straight leg up off the floor approximately 12 inches and hold.

4. Repeat ten times, then change legs.

Plank

Photo 31 shows the plank.

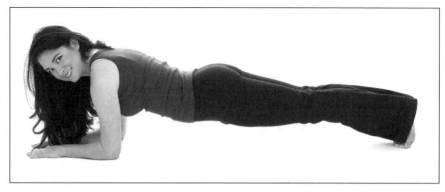

Photo 31

1. Lie down on your stomach and brace the core muscles.

2. Raise your body up on your toes and elbows.

3. Lower your buttocks down until level with your shoulders. Squeeze your navel toward your spine. This is the key to this exercise and really works the core. Make sure your buttocks are not sticking up.

4. Hold for 30 seconds and increase the hold to two minutes as you improve. Alternatively, you can hold for ten seconds and repeat ten times.

Note that the plank can be modified from toes to knees. If you find it difficult to do the plank while resting on your toes (as you may if your upper body strength is not enough to hold you up), you can still work your core by balancing on your knees instead of your toes. When your core and upper body strength increase, you can return to doing the plank while resting on your toes.

Side Plank

Photo 32 shows the side plank.

Photo 32

1. Lie on your side and brace your core muscles.
2. Raise yourself up on the side of one foot and your elbow.
3. Raise your trunk off the floor. Do not let your middle sag. Squeeze your obliques. (The obliques, which are the muscles that cover the sides of your body, were discussed earlier in this chapter.)
4. Hold for 30 seconds and increase the hold to two minutes as you improve. Alternatively, you can hold for ten seconds and repeat ten times.

Note that the side plank can be modified by supporting your legs with your knees. Again, if your upper body is not strong enough at this point to support you as you balance on your elbow and foot, you can try supporting your lower body with your knee first by bending your knees and resting your weight on them.

Superman (and Woman!)

Photo 33 shows the Superman.

Photo 33

1. While laying flat on the floor, brace your trunk.
2. Extend your arms above your head.
3. Raise your arms and legs off the floor simultaneously.
4. Repeat ten times.

FITNESS TO GO: YOUR KNEES

Your knees are biomechanical wonders, yet the key to your knees are your quadriceps. The quads are the four large muscles in the front of your legs. They control how much pressure your knees and kneecaps experience with every step. Strong quads can prevent many knee conditions that athletes and active agers experience. The quads are the first place I look for weakness when patients come to my office with knee pain. Keeping your quads strong is an easy addition to your daily life and can be as simple as leaning up against a wall, as shown in the following exercise.

Short Arc Squats/Wall Slides

Short arc squats/wall slides, shown in Photo 34, are good for your quadriceps, buttocks, and core.

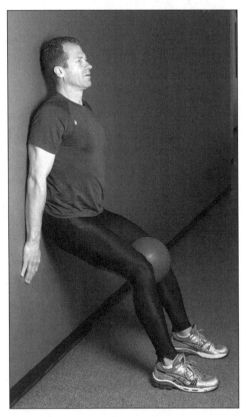

Photo 34

1. Stand with your back up against a wall and your legs shoulder width apart. Place two rolled towels or a medicine ball between your knees.

2. Brace your core and pull your navel toward your spine.

3. While keeping your core engaged, slowly slide your back down the wall until your knees are bent to approximately 60 degrees. This is just shy of parallel to the floor. Limiting the knee bend will decrease the pressure on your knees and still work your quads.

4. Hold in the bent position for ten seconds and repeat ten times. Do two sets.

Straight Leg Raises

Photos 35 and 36 show straight leg raises, which work the quadriceps, hip flexors, and core.

Photo 35

Photo 36

1. Lying flat on your back, engage your core.

2. Bend one leg up at the knee and keep the other leg straight.

3. Still lying flat on your back, using the straight leg, tighten the right quad (front of thigh) and raise your leg up off the floor until your thighs are parallel. Hold this position five seconds and then lower your leg until it almost touches the floor. Be careful not to let your back sway up off the floor.

4. Repeat ten times. Do two sets and then switch to the other leg.

5. To increase the difficulty, you can repeat the sets while supporting yourself on your elbows (Photo 35) or hands (Photo 36).

FITNESS TO GO: YOUR SHOULDERS

Shoulder pain and irritation or tears of your rotator cuff (the muscles that make your shoulders stable) are very common after 40. We never think about our shoulders until they are keeping us up at night, and then they are all we can think about. The problem is that when most of us go to the gym, we only work those big cosmetic muscles we can see—the biceps, triceps, and chest—but while these are great to look at, they are not the key players in shoulder health or sports.

A few simple exercises can mean the difference between painless, strong shoulders and agonizing shoulder pain. These are the same exercises you need to recover from rotator cuff pain, so keep them handy. You can perform these with exercise bands or light dumbbells. The resistance should be enough that you feel a slight burn in your muscles but not more. Remember that you want to use only your shoulder for this series of exercises. If you are using so much resistance that you find yourself using your whole back to pull the band or lift the weight, it is too much. You will know you are using your back and trunk if they move or jerk when you are lifting your arm.

Arm Raises

Photos 37, 38, and 39 show three types of arm raises, in three directions: lateral, forward, and across the body.

1. Stand with your feet shoulder width apart. Engage your core (every exercise can be a core exercise). Place one end of an exercise band under your right foot, and hold the opposite end with your right hand. Slowly raise your arm to the side until your arm is level with your shoulder (Photo 37). Hold

Photo 37   Photo 38   Photo 39

for five seconds. Slowly lower your arm. Repeat this ten times. Do two sets.

2. Repeat the arm raises with your arm raised in front of you (Photo 38). Be aware of your back. You should be using only your shoulder to raise the band and not leaning backward to raise your arm. Hold five seconds and lower slowly. Repeat ten times. Do two sets.

3. Next, place the band under your left foot and continue to hold the band with your right hand. Raise your arm across your body in a V motion until it is parallel with your shoulder (Photo 39). Hold five seconds and slowly lower your arm. Repeat ten times. Do two sets.

4. Repeat these three exercises with the band in your left hand.

External and Internal Rotation

Photos 40, 41, and 42 show external and internal rotation, which work the infraspinatus and subscapularis muscles.

1. For external rotation, place one end of an exercise band around a sturdy object, such as a doorknob, and stand with your left side toward the door. Place the other end of the band in your right hand (Photo 40).

2. Pull the band away from your body with your elbow against your left side. Repeat this ten times. Do two sets.

3. For internal rotation, place the band in your right hand and pull it across your body with your right elbow against your right side (Photos 41 and 42). Repeat this ten times. Do two sets.

4. Turn your body so that your right side is toward the door and repeat with the other arms.

5. Keep your elbow close to your side during these exercises.

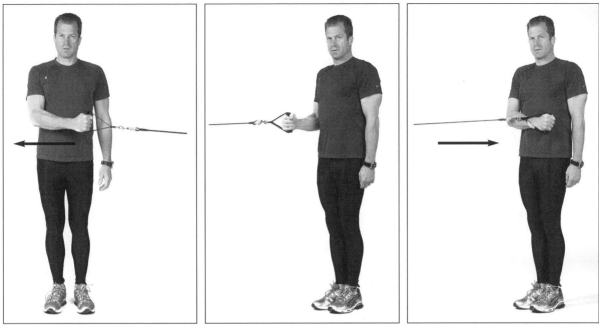

Photo 40 (rotate arm out—external)   Photo 41   Photo 42 (rotate arm internally across body)

FITNESS TO GO: YOUR LEGS

You may not even notice the muscles in the lower part of your legs—that is, until one of them is irritated or inflamed. Weakness in the lower legs can mean pain with each step, or sport-halting injury. Shin splints, calf pulls, Achilles tendonitis, and peroneal tendonitis (behind the outer ankles) can be avoided with these simple exercises. If you pay some attention to them, it is easy to keep these forgotten muscles happy and working hard for you.

Plantar Flexion/Dorsiflexion

Photos 43, 44, 45, and 46 show plantar flexion and dorsiflexion, which work the calves and anterior tibialis muscles.

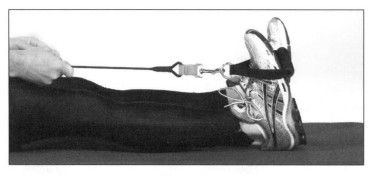

Photo 43

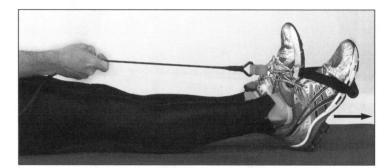

Photo 44 (foot presses forward)

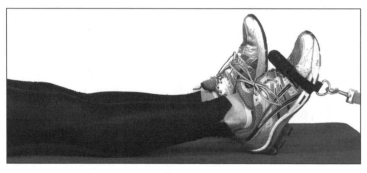

Photo 45

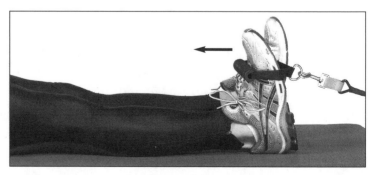

Photo 46 (pull foot back)

1. Sit on the floor and place a rolled up towel under your ankle and lower calf.

2. To strengthen your calves (plantar flexion), secure the end of an exercise band around the ball of your foot, and hold the other end with your hands (Photo 43).

3. Press forward on the band like you are stepping on the gas pedal of your car, and hold for five seconds (Photo 44). Repeat until your calf is fatigued. Switch sides.

4. To work the front of your legs or your anterior tibialis muscle (dorsiflexion), remain sitting on the floor with a towel rolled up under your ankle. Secure one end of the band around a sturdy object, and place the other end around the ball of your foot (Photo 45).

5. Pull your foot back toward your head and hold for five seconds (Photo 46). Repeat this until the front of your leg is fatigued. Switch sides.

Inversion/Eversion

Photos 47 and 48 show inversion/eversion, which work the peroneal and posterior tibalis muscles.

1. Sit on the floor and place a rolled up towel under your ankle and lower calf.

2. To work the posterior peroneal muscles through inversion (which means moving your toes and foot toward the midline of your body, or in other words, toward your other foot), secure one end of an exercise band to a sturdy object and the other end around the ball of your foot. The band should be stretching away from your body as shown in Photo 47.

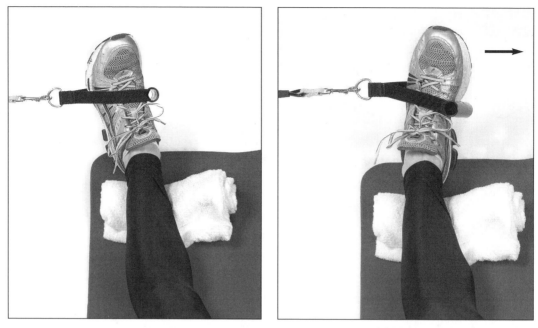

Photo 47   Photo 48 (foot moves in)

3. Using only your foot and ankle, not your whole leg, pull the band in toward the middle of your body (Photo 48) and hold five seconds. Repeat this until fatigue sets in.

4. To work the outside of your leg, or peroneal muscles, simply change positions so that the band is stretching in front of your body.

5. Using only your foot and ankle and not your whole leg, evert or pull the band so that your foot moves out away from the middle of your body. Hold your foot everted for five seconds and repeat until you are fatigued.

Even though these leg-strengthening exercises all use exercise bands, you can strengthen your lower legs (and prevent muscle imbalance and shin splints) without any equipment at all. The goal is to strengthen the muscles that dorsiflex (bring up) and plantarflex (lower) your ankles. You can do these exercises in your office, at the airport, or in the kitchen while cooking.

Wall Shin Raises

1. Stand with your back and shoulders against the wall, with your feet shoulder width apart and about one foot in front of the wall.

2. Raise your toes as high off the ground toward your body as you can with your weight on your heels.

3. Slowly lower your toes until they are almost but not quite on the floor, and then flex them up again. Repeat this ten times.

You will feel the burn in your anterior tibialis muscle in the front of your shin. As you get better at this exercise, you can "pulse" quickly from flexing up and extending your ankle down.

Once you can comfortably complete the wall shin raise with both legs (both basic and quick), progress to the single-leg wall shin raise. The basic position for this exercise is the same as for the double-leg raise, except that you begin with only one foot in contact with the ground and the other foot resting lightly on the wall behind you. Now, as you carry out the overall routine, your full body weight is on one foot, as it is during running, and the exercises are considerably more difficult.

Heel Step Downs

Heel step downs are a great exercise for preventing shin splints.

1. Stand with your feet together and take a natural step forward.

2. As you heel strikes the floor in front of you, prevent your foot from flexing down as you transfer your weight forward. This

forces your anterior tibialis muscles to contract as they lengthen and mimics the foot action during running.

3. Return your foot to the starting position, and repeat on the other side.

4. Perform ten of these step downs on each side.

5. When you have mastered this with short strides, you can increase your stride length to make the exercise more difficult.

TOO MUCH IN ONE WEEK?

I know this seems like a lot of exercises to do three times a week, but if you do one body part at a time and spread the entire regimen throughout your day, it will seem effortless. For instance, you can work your quadriceps with straight leg raises before you get out of bed in the morning, do your shoulders while standing in your office talking on the phone, or do the planks after your aerobic workout. You can fit it all in because these exercises are fit to go!

At this point, you have a vision of what your physical future can look like, you know how you are different now than you were before, and you are equipped to flex, move, and carry a load. In Chapter 7, you will learn the skill of staying upright.

HOME**WORK**

Go to your local sporting goods store and get two sets of resistance tubing. Usually, a set includes different strengths, but if not, test them out in the store and choose the one that gives you a moderate amount of resistance. Place one set wherever you spend the most time in your home (kitchen, TV room, garage) and take the other to work. If you travel for a living, stick the type you are currently using in your briefcase. You are more likely to do the exercises if the tubing is readily available.

"There will come a point in the race, when you alone will need to decide. You will need to make a choice. Do you really want it? You will need to decide."

—Rolf Arands, editor, *Runner's Gazette*

CHAPTER SEVEN

F.A.C.E.

*Your Future by Keeping Your E—
Equilibrium/Balance*

Don't fall down. Easy advice to give, but in reality—in your 40s, 50s, 60s, and beyond—it is not always easy to stay upright. Even if you have not fallen in years, it is likely that you will in the future. Did you know that after age 25, your balance begins to decline, and that after 65, one in three people will fall doing normal activities of daily living? Falls in the later years often result in wrist and hip fractures, which can have a devastating effect on your lifestyle or even threaten your life.

Even if you have mastered the other three components of F.A.C.E.-ing your future, you must never ignore equilibrium and balance, which is an important component of fitness after 40. Balance is important for not only improving sports performance but even for the mundane activities of life.

SYSTEMS AT WORK

Have you ever stood on the deck of a boat and felt the sway of the water? In order to stay upright, your body is sensing the direction of the sway and activating the muscles on the opposite side of the body to contract and correct your upright position. Your muscles and joints "know" where they are in space. This process, which is called proprioception, happens at lightening speed without your consciously thinking about it. Proprioception is the ability of our bodies to detect where we are in space (i.e., whether we are leaning to the right or left) and to contract muscles appropriately for us to stay upright.

There are actually many systems working together to keep us standing upright. Balancing effectively takes our eyes, ears (vestibular system), and peripheral sensory system (skin receptors of pressure and touch) as well as our neuromuscular connections (the nerve pathways between our brains and muscles, tendons, ligaments, and joints). Our brains are able to coordinate these signals to determine where our limbs are in space and the speed and direction of their movement.

With aging, these systems may become less functional, which can lead to imbalance. Our brains miscalculate our position and make errors in determining where our limbs are because the signals our brains receive are less accurate. As our vision and peripheral senses decline, we engage our leg muscles more to prevent sway. To cope, the hip girdle, quadriceps, and muscles surrounding the ankles are engaged to stiffen and freeze the lower legs for upright standing. Since it involves our muscles so much, balance is another reason that maintaining muscle strength is key.

Declines in proprioception and balance are also seen in people who suffer ligament injuries or have osteoarthritis (the "wear and tear" type of arthritis). I did a study of Senior Olympians that showed that people with wear and tear arthritis of the knee are more likely to have injuries than those who were not diagnosed with arthritis. In addition, we know from multiple studies that if you have arthritis in one knee, not only does your balance decline in that knee but it will also decline in the other knee. The reason for this is not clear, but what is clear is that balance and proprioception can be retrained. This is important, since poor balance not only leads to falls but may lead to increased injury.

The good news is that the neuromuscular connections can be entirely reclaimed by specific daily attention. Falls can be prevented. A large analysis of balance studies found that muscle strengthening and balance retraining programs can decrease the risk of falls by 45 percent. In addition, studies show that people who practice the noncompetitive martial art of tai chi (which emphasizes gentle movements and stretching) have a significantly better sense of joint position and better reaction times than people of the same age who did not practice such balance-intense activities.

Aging golfers show the same retention of balance-sense and reaction time as practitioners of tai chi. This makes sense since a good golf swing requires not only good balance, with precise control of the head and body in relationship to the legs, but coordinated muscle activity throughout the swing. Overall fitness and lower extremity muscle strength are important determinants of remaining balanced. Just like any component of fitness, "if you don't use it, you lose it," and—in terms of equilibrium—you can be older than your years.

On the first day of my 12-week PRIMA START programs, I always talk to our "Starters" about F.A.C.E.-ing their futures and the four components of fitness after 40. They are surprised when I talk about balance and equilibrium. Many don't realize that their balance is not what it once was until we begin to do some of the warm-up exercises that require standing on one foot. Immediately their arms are spread out trying to balance on the ground like they were on a tightrope wire. We lose our balance subtly, and don't realize it until we are toppling over. This may be the case for you, too, but it is easy to find out what the state of your neuromuscular connections are.

TEST YOURSELF

You don't have to be falling all around like Jerry's klutzy neighbor Kramer on *Seinfeld* to have a balance problem. Let's test you right now:

1. Stand next to a firm surface such as a counter or chair back.
2. Hold your hands above the surface in case you need support.
3. Close your eyes and lift one foot off the ground.
4. Balance on the other foot.
5. Count out loud the number of seconds you are able to balance.

The shorter your balance time, the "older" your equilibrium is. If you balanced for more than 22 seconds, your balance is as young as a 20-year-old's; 15 seconds, you have the balance of a 30-year-old; 7.2 seconds, of a 40-year-old; 3.7 seconds, of a 50-year-old; and if you toppled over right away, you are 60 in "balance years."

If you are fit and strong, you can have better balance than much younger sedentary people. There are many ways you can boost your balance.

Balance Boosters

- *Stay strong*. Strengthening your buttocks, quadriceps, and hamstrings go a long way in improving balance.

- *Join a class*. Tai chi, yoga, and pilates all require slow deliberate movements, trunk rotation, and one-legged stances.

- *Be productive in your down time*. Between sets of strength exercises, while brushing your teeth in the morning, or while waiting at a street corner for the light to change, try standing on one leg and balancing.

- *Work balance exercises into your daily routine*. You don't need any special equipment—just your body. For best results, do some or all of these exercises every day. It takes four to 12 weeks of work to see a result. (Before beginning all these exercises, first engage your core muscles.)

BALANCE EXERCISES

The Stork

This exercise, shown in Photo 49, is simple and highly versatile. You can do it while standing anywhere—at the sink while washing dishes, at your desk while you talk on the phone, while brushing your teeth, or between sets of strength exercises.

1. Stand with your feet slightly apart and raise one leg off the ground while keeping your arms to the sides and your shoulders relaxed (Photo 49).

2. Try to balance for 30 seconds. Repeat two times, then switch legs.

3. Try to work up to two minutes.

4. If you have difficulty balancing with no hands, try placing your fingertips or one fingertip on a hard surface until you are able to balance with no hands. Try and relax—it makes it easier.

You can make this exercise more difficult by closing your eyes while you balance. Removing vision from the picture requires more work from your muscles. Here are some other variations on the stork:

- Once you have mastered standing still as a stork, try swinging your arms like you are running in place.

- When this is easy, hold water bottles or light weights in your hands and swing them (see Photo 50).

Photo 49   Photo 50

- To make the stork even more challenging, fold up a bath towel so that it is several inches thick and do the stork while standing on it. Be careful not to cheat by gripping the floor or the towel with your toes.

- If you are a golfer, mix in the stork to balance your golf swing by taking your address position for a normal short iron shot and slowly lifting your right foot off the ground while maintaining your spine angle. Hold your foot four inches off the ground for 30 seconds and then lower it. Repeat this on the left side.

Toe Raise

1. Stand with your shoulders over your hips, hips over your knees, knees over your ankles . . . in other words, line up.

2. Focus your eyes on a spot on the ground 25 degrees in front of you.

3. While you stay focused on the spot, raise up onto your toes using the whole surface of your foot.

4. Lift the weight off your heels and ball of your foot onto our toes.

5. Move slowly and in a controlled way without jerking from side to side.

6. Repeat 10 to 15 times.

7. If you need some support doing this exercise, stand behind a chair and use your fingertips to balance yourself.

Hip Flexors

1. Stand next to a sturdy surface like a chair. If you need to use your fingertips for balance, do so.

2. Raise one leg off the floor like you are marching slowly, then lower it.

3. Do not bend forward at the waist (engage your core).

4. Repeat 10 to 15 times on each leg.

5. Make this more difficult by removing your fingertips from the chair (if you are using it) and even more difficult by closing your eyes.

Side Leg Raise

1. Stand next to a sturdy surface like a chair. If you need to use your fingertips for balance, do so.

2. Raise one leg off the floor to the side and hold it six to 12 inches off the floor, then lower it (Photo 51).

Photo 51

3. Do not bend forward at the waist (engage your core).

4. Repeat ten to 15 times on each leg.

5. Make this more difficult by removing your fingertips from the chair (if you are using it) and even more difficult by closing your eyes.

Walk the Line

This can be difficult even when sober, especially with your eyes closed.

1. Choose a straight line in front of you like a tile floor and walk, one foot directly in front of the other, along it. Try this first with your arms extended out to the side for balance, and then with your arms at your sides.

2. Walk backward to the starting point, still along the straight line.

3. When this is easy, do it with your eyes closed.

EXTRA FOR EXPERTS

You probably think the balance exercises described here sound simple, and you are right. They are simple, yet I think many people will be surprised by how wobbly they are when they try them. Once you have the simple balance exercises under control, you can progress to more dynamic balance challenges using physioballs or BOSU balls. BOSU balls are pieces of exercise equipment that look like half a beach ball on a round plate. Performing any of the balancing exercises described above gets harder when you are engaging your whole core and body by standing on a BOSU ball.

Here are some extra balance exercises for experts.

CHOP Progression

1. Stand with your legs shoulder width apart and hold a medicine ball or dumbbell over your head.

2. Lower the ball or weight down between your knees in a squatting motion, keeping your back straight.

3. Raise the ball or weight back up over your head.

4. Take the ball or weight from high right to low left and then from low right to high left.

5. Repeat these three movements 10 to 15 times.

To make this even harder, perform this exercise while standing on a BOSU ball. If you are really expert, close your eyes.

Cone Touch

1. Place an object about waist high one yard in front of you.

2. Stand on one leg and reach and touch the object while maintaining your balance.

3. Repeat this 10 to 15 times, then switch legs.

To make this exercise harder, lower the height of the object in front of you or stand on a BOSU ball.

You can do these balance exercises between parts of your resistance work (the "C" part of F.A.C.E.—carrying a load). If you do, you should follow the order of balance—resistance—balance—resistance—balance. By doing so, you have killed two birds with one stone. You are getting two of the F.A.C.E. components of fitness in during the same time period instead of doing resistance—rest—resistance—rest, or doing balance—rest—balance—rest, in two separate time periods. You are doing resistance—balance—resistance—balance. You can do this because the balance exercises are not strenuous and probably don't require rest in between.

Equilibrium and balance are easy to ignore until you need them, and then it is way too late. Because the last thing anyone needs is to fall down, it pays to take the time to test your balance (using the balance test in this chapter) and use a few of the balance boosters given here every day.

WHAT YOU'VE GAINED SO FAR

Now you have covered the four components of fitness after 40 and are ready to F.A.C.E. your future in a smart way. It seems like a lot, but it will seem less overwhelming once you work the exercises into your muscle memory (yes, your muscles have memory and your mind will remember how it feels to do the exercises), know your target heart rate range, and know how much weight you should be carrying.

I hope what you have gained is not simply a list of exercises to perform but a real understanding of why you are going to do them. I will help you put it all together in Chapter 14 and you will close this book with a plan for fitness after 40.

H O M E**W O R K**

Before moving on, take a minute and perform the balance test in this chapter. How old is your balance? If you felt wobbly during the test, seize the moment and perform one of the balance exercises described above. Make this your daily investment into standing upright.

"Those who think they have no time for bodily exercise will sooner or later have to find time for illness."

—British statesman Edward Stanley (1826–1893), from "The Conduct of Life," a speech given in 1873

CHAPTER EIGHT

Wear, Tear, Repair

"I had been trying to do the same kind of workouts that I did in high school, and I was constantly getting strains and pains. I spent 50 percent of my time healing from my workouts."

I have heard variations of this statement from many of my patients. Either they do the same kinds of workouts they have always done, or they cram all their exercising into the weekend. These "weekend warriors" try to make exercise-cramming work for them because their weeks are crazy . . . activities, errands, and no scheduled time for exercise. When the weekend comes, they are free and they hit the gym or road or courts with bravado. They ignore the fact that such a dramatic shift from in-activity to activity makes them prone to injury. Come Monday morning, these warriors are speed-dialing my office for an appointment. This was especially true during the Olympics in Beijing. People were so inspired, they flew out their doors to exercise. Many ended up in our office because you cannot regain your youth in a few days.

Sports injuries are way up for baby boomers. According to the Consumer Product Safety Commission, there was a 33 percent increase in the number of sports injuries in mature athletes between 1991 and 1998. The highest number of injuries occurred while people were biking, playing basketball, playing baseball, and running, with the most common injuries in the ankle/leg, knee, shoulder, and lower back. Acute and overuse injuries are the primary reasons people stop exercising and the major causes of performance declines in masters athletes. The

PRECAUTIONS YOU SHOULD TAKE WHEN BEGINNING TO EXERCISE

- Don't be a "weekend warrior," packing a week's worth of activity into a day or two. Try to maintain a moderate level of activity throughout the week.

- Learn to do your sport right. Using proper form can reduce your risk of overuse injuries, such as tendonitis and stress fractures.

- Remember safety gear. Depending on the sport, this may mean knee or wrist pads or a helmet.

- Increase your exercise level gradually.

- Strive for a total body workout of cardiovascular, strength training, and flexibility and equilibrium exercises.

- Engage in cross-training. Mixing up activities like running, swimming, cycling, and rowing reduces injury while promoting total fitness.

more we push the athletic envelope—whether we are longtime competitors or the sudden athlete leaping off the couch for the first time in years—injuries are always lurking in the wings, ready to sideline us if we don't learn to avoid them.

INJURIES IN MASTERS ATHLETES

In 2001, the University of Pittsburgh conducted a survey of more than 2,500 Senior Olympians at the National Summer Senior Games. A majority of the athletes—89 percent—had experienced at least one sports-related injury since turning 50, and more than 50 percent had experienced up to five injuries. These injuries did not occur just because of a bad landing or acute incident. In fact, the majority of injuries in senior athletes are the result of overuse: workouts that are too frequent, too repetitive, and too intense. During the 2001 Senior Olympics, more than 60 percent of the injuries were attributed to overuse. Such problems commonly occur at the insertions of tendons into bone. In addition, 23 percent of the injuries were the result of falls. The athletes who reported having arthritis were twice as likely to have more than five injuries as athletes without the disease. They were also three times more likely to report knee injuries.

For aging athletes and adult onset exercisers, the main problems reported are acute muscle strains and chronic tendonitis. The junction between the tendon and the muscle is especially vulnerable since the structure of the muscle is less "stretchy" in this area than in the middle of the muscle. In addition, when muscles are fatigued, they lose their ability to absorb energy and are less coordinated. This makes them susceptible to injury during so-called eccentric movement. ("Eccentric" means that the muscle is contracting as it is lengthening. This predisposes it to injury.)

Too much, too soon, too often, and with too little rest—these terrible toos predispose us to overuse injuries. Unfortunately, these problems are common in older athletes and often result from a condition called tendonosis. While tendonitis is the acute inflammation of the tendon, tendonosis is the longer term, cumulative effect of repetitive microtrauma to the tendon that does not properly heal.

The Achilles tendon, patellar tendon, rotator cuff tendons, medial epicondylitis (inside elbow), lateral epicondylitis (tennis elbow), and wrist tendons are all more vulnerable with aging. Remember that in Chapter 2, we discussed the fact that as we age, our cells and tissues have less regenerative capacity than when we were younger. This leads to less durability of our muscles and tendons. Our musculoskeletal tissues also have a lower healing capacity, so it takes longer to recover between intense workouts. When not rehabilitated correctly, these overuse injuries can linger on and on, resulting in literally years of lost activity. This simply points to the fact we have been making through out this book: As we age, we must not only become or remain active but be smarter about how we do it and F.A.C.E. our physical futures.

I experienced this myself as I aged. When I turned 30 and was only running, I developed a number of persistent injuries. I could almost predict that when I reached a certain level of training, I would pull my medial calf muscle or get hip pain. The muscle pulls often set me back a couple of weeks, which can devastate a race training schedule. At age 40, I ramped up my training while also working on flexibility, lifting weights, and cross-training. I did not get hurt at all and managed to cut almost two minutes from my mile time.

You may have also experienced the pop, tear, and pain that sidelines you and leaves you wondering how in the world it happened or what to do next.

HOW YOU HEAL

From the moment a ligament, muscle, or tendon tears, your body goes to work to repair the damage. Here's what happens at each stage of the healing process:

- *At the moment of injury:* Chemicals are released from damaged cells, triggering a process called inflammation. Blood vessels at the injury site become dilated. Blood flow increases to carry nutrients to the site of the tissue damage.

- *Within hours of injury:* White blood cells (leukocytes) travel down the bloodstream to the injury site, either inside your body or on your skin, where they begin to tear down and remove damaged tissue, allowing other specialized cells to start developing scar tissue. Scar tissue is not the perfect way for us to heal; however, it is the way we do it. Only the bones are capable of regenerating without scars. All other soft tissues heal well but with scar tissue.

- *Within days of injury:* Scar tissue is beginning to form. The amount of scarring may be proportional to the amount of swelling, inflammation, or bleeding within. In the next few weeks, the damaged area will regain a great deal of strength as scar tissue continues to mature.

- *Within a month of injury:* Scar tissue may start to shrink, bringing damaged, torn, or separated tissues back together. However, it may be several months or more before the injury is completely healed.

WHAT DO WE DO WHEN WE GET INJURED?

Treating injuries begins before you get injured. Overtraining and overuse are the most common reasons for getting injured. Your muscles get tired during workouts and become inflamed and may feel sore. Your muscles and the tendons that hold them to the bone need time between intense workouts to recover adequately. By ignoring the ache, you are predisposing the formation of scar tissue from the persistent inflammation caused by too frequent workouts. Scarred tissue is more fragile than healthy tissue.

Here are the four rules to follow in injury prevention:

1. *Rule Number 1* in preventing overuse injury is to exercise intensely every *other* day to give your body time to recover.

2. *Rule Number 2* is to mix up your workout to use different muscle groups. In other words, cross-train.

3. *Rule Number 3* is to warm up before exercising. This is as easy as using the dynamic warm-up in Chapter 5 or walking for ten minutes before you run, or setting the resistance on the stair stepper on low before you ramp up your workout. (Remember that the warm-up is not stretching but is separate. Also recall that we do not stretch prior to the warm-up). You are simply trying to raise your core body temperature. Warm muscles and tendons are less brittle than cold muscles. The flexibility exercises in Chapter 4 are also a good way to pre-vent injury. While you do not want to stretch when cold, the stretches you perform daily will keep your body limber and prevent scar formation during the exercise recovery period. The proper order for initiating a workout is to warm up, stretch, then turn up the intensity.

As I mentioned, the most common injuries I see in senior athletes are to the leg and ankle, knee, shoulder, and lower back. Treating these injuries is preventing these injuries. The way we do this is called *Pre-hab*. Pre-hab is simply strengthening the most injury-prone muscle groups before they ever get injured. The Fitness to Go section in Chapter 6 is all about Pre-habbing these four common injuries. The stronger our muscles are, the less likely they are to succumb to injury; therefore, strengthening our weak areas is key.

   4. *Rule Number 4* for injury prevention, therefore, is Pre-hab!

TREATING MINOR INJURIES WITH R.I.C.E.

Each letter of this acronym stands for one component of treating minor injuries.

- *R = Rest*. After you hurt yourself, back off the intensity of your workouts and give your injured part a rest. This does not mean sitting around on a couch. Rest is an active process and may involve changing activities; you can cycle, swim, or walk instead of running. It may also require taking a day or so off. While you are resting, make sure you keep moving your injured joint and continue gently stretching your injured muscles. This will prevent healing with scar tissue and stiffness.

- *I = Ice*. So good for injury—what would we do without it? Place a bag of ice or an ice pack over your injured part and leave it there for 20 minutes several times a day during your recovery period, especially in the first 72 hours. An easy way to do this is to put the ice in a thin plastic bag (the kind from the grocery store work well) and strap it on with clear plastic wrap. Note that this is not the time for heat. Use heat only after the first 72 hours to warm the injured body part up prior to motion.

- *C = Compression*. This is just what it sounds like. This will do wonders for preventing and reducing swelling. Keep a couple of Ace Wraps around the house for just this purpose. When you get injured, gently wrap the Ace around the joint, starting farthest away from your heart and wrapping toward your heart. This will help your body absorb the fluid causing the swelling and move it back into your circulation instead of getting pooled (accumulated) at the injury site. This will also help you recover faster since your body must eventually reabsorb all the fluid it dumps at the injury site.

- *E = Elevate*. Coupled with compression, raising an injured part as high as you can above your heart prevents and reduces swelling. When hurt, we temporarily lose our ability to control fluid at the injury site and so must help our bodies. If we don't elevate, fluid will pool at the injury site, making healing more difficult.

So what if Rules 1 to 4 given above didn't prevent your injury? Now what? Stop playing or exercising immediately. Ice the injured area as soon as you can, and elevate the body part above your heart. These measures will help minimize the amount of swelling and inflammation that occurs and will decrease the pain. Taking an NSAID (non-steroidal anti-inflammatory drug) such as ibuprofen or naprosyn will also decrease inflammation and pain. Ice and elevation are key in the first 72 hours after injury. This is not the time to put heat on your injury.

Next, you should temporarily back off your activity level. This does not mean that you sit on the couch! Getting back in the game is an active process. However, if you are unable to bear weight on the limb you hurt or can't move the joint, you should see your doctor.

Even if your injury is minor, your body will still try and protect itself by getting stiff. Gently move the joint through its full range of motion, fully straight and fully bent. Do this several times a day. Gentle stretching will aid in the healing of a pulled muscle with less scar tissue. While you are recovering from your injury, you also can still maintain your fitness by working the other body parts that remain well. For instance, if you hurt your shoulder, you can still use a stationary bike; if you hurt your leg, you can lift weights with your arms or swim with a buoy between your legs.

When I rehabilitate one of my surgery patients, I follow a specific rehab order for returning him to sport. This order is the same for getting you back into the game. Regain your full range of motion first. When this is back, you may begin strengthening the muscle you pulled or the muscles around the joint you injured. At the same time, you should focus on training your injured joint to balance again. We lose our ability to balance well when we are injured. This is especially true for our knees and ankles.

SPORT-SPECIFIC SETBACKS

Running

The common ground among running injuries is that many result from too much road pounding. Remember the terrible toos discussed earlier in this chapter: too much, too soon, too often, too little rest? Runners are especially susceptible to them. Another reason this group gets injured is that almost all of the runners I encounter only run. They don't do anything to

ACUTE AND CHRONIC INJURIES

Acute injuries, such as sprained ankles, strained backs, or fractured hands, occur suddenly during activity. Signs of acute injury include:

- Sudden, severe pain
- Swelling
- Inability to place weight on a lower limb
- Extreme tenderness in an upper limb
- Inability to move a joint through its full range of motion
- Extreme limb weakness
- Visible dislocation or break of the bone

Chronic injuries usually result from overusing one area of the body while playing a sport or exercising over a long period. These injuries creep up on you and you may not be able to pinpoint the exact time they began. Signs of chronic injury include:

- Pain that increases when performing an activity
- A dull ache when at rest
- Swelling and redness

strengthen their cores or buttocks, let alone stretch their hamstrings or other leg muscles.

The most common running injuries are bursitis over your hip bone (ITB syndrome), anterior knee pain, Achilles tendonitis, shin splints, and plantar fasciitis (sharp heel pain when you first get out of bed in the morning). What you need to remember is that we are a kinetic chain from our toes to our backs; in other words, everything is connected and works together. This means that even something simple like having a stiff big toe that will not flex when you roll through a stride can force your weight to the outside of your foot, which changes the forces across your knee while bending it by pulling your kneecap to the outside. This increased patellar force can put too much pressure on the kneecap cartilage or on the patellar tendon below the kneecap and cause them to become irritated. The pain is worse when your quadriceps are not strong enough to keep the kneecap on straight. Tight hamstrings can cause you to have a shorter stride or walk with bent knees. This will force your hips to bend more and may cause low back pain. We really are all connected.

So what does a runner have to do to stay injury-free? Start with your big toe. Flex it up and down and move it all around in a circle. To land correctly, you need 70 degrees of flexibility in the big toe. Next, make sure your calves, hamstrings, and quads are well stretched. Our muscles are most efficient and most supple at their optimum length. Next, even runners need to work on keeping their legs, hips, and cores strong. Use the Fitness to Go section of Chapter 6 as a start.

Photo 52

For one simple exercise for your lower body, try the prisoner squat, shown in Photo 52.

1. Stand with your feet a little farther than shoulder width apart and squat down with your knees above your ankles.

2. Keep your back straight and your head up. This will strengthen your quads, buttocks, and core.

3. Try ten squats several times a day.

You can work an upper body workout into the prisoner squat by standing with both feet on an exercise band and holding one end in each hand. As you do the prisoner squat, pull the band up to your shoulders. If you face your palms forward and pull the band above your shoulders, you will be working your back. Alternatively, with palms facing toward you and elbows in, you can curl your biceps.

Finally, don't forget your most important piece of equipment for runners: the shoes. When your shoes are too old, they no longer support your efforts. Even if the upper cloth part of your shoes still looks good, realize that the soles last only 350–500 miles before their engineering fails. It works well to have several pairs that you rotate through instead of completely wearing out a pair before having to break in another. Chapter 12 tells you how to think about purchasing shoes.

SUDDEN RUNNER'S SYNDROME

Those of you just starting out or the weekend warriors who "start out" every weekend are especially prone to a sudden onset of new leg pain, which takes the form of muscle soreness and tendonitis. Your muscles and tendons are probably wondering what they ever did to you to deserve such pounding. They scream back by getting all hot, bothered, and sore.

As adults, most of us develop the delayed muscle soreness from sudden increases in exercise intensity two days after the workout day. The first day after, you feel a little muscle burn, but the real hobbling soreness comes 48 hours later. Muscle soreness is caused by the accumulation of multiple microtears in your muscle fibers during exercise. These tears form in proportion to the amount and type of exercise you are doing. Eccentric muscle contractions—those contractions that force the muscle to lengthen as it is firing—cause the most microtears. Examples of eccentric contractions include running downhill or down stairs and the lowering of weights. Soreness also occurs due to the buildup of lactic acid. Lactic acid, which is the byproduct of anaerobic (without oxygen) metabolism, builds up in our muscles under intense conditions.

Muscle soreness generally fades away in a few days. In the meantime, you should recover actively. Drink a lot of water immediately after exercise, and cool down actively to wash the lactic acid out of your muscles (for instance, walk after you run to cool down). Instead of exercising intensely the next day (which I never recommend), take a walk or do a low-impact workout, making sure to gently stretch after you warm up, or get a massage. Not only does massage feel good but it can reduce some of the swelling that causes the muscle pain. Ice and NSAIDs can also take the edge off the muscle soreness and inflammation. As your soreness fades, warm up well and resume your exercise.

As discussed previously, tendonitis is the inflammation of overworked tendons. For sudden onset runners (and swimmers and cyclists, for that matter), acute tendonitis from sudden increases in activity intensity can slowly progress to tendonosis. Tendonosis is chronic structural changes to the tendon, when the normally white, gleaming, pulled-taffy appearance of the tendon is changed to a gray, amorphous, painful lump. The best treatment for tendonitis is prevention. Don't just A.C.E. your future: You must F.A.C.E. it. In other words, flexibility is key.

Finally, sudden onset exercisers can quickly develop muscle imbalances that lead to injury. Shin splints are one of the most common muscle imbalance injuries. You know, the aching down the front of your legs that hurts with each step. Go to the Fitness to Go section of Chapter 6 and look at the leg exercises to learn how to avoid shin splints. If you do get them, treat them initially with an ice massage, active rest, and NSAIDs. To perform an ice massage, freeze water in a paper cup. Then tear back the cup edges to expose about an inch of ice, which should be rubbed over the front of the legs.

Swimming

While swimming is an excellent way to stay in shape and avoid the pounding of the road, aging shoulders are very susceptible to rotator cuff injury. The rotator cuff lives in a house of bone. That is, the main rotator cuff tendon, the supraspinatus (above the spine of the shoulder blade), travels under a ceiling of bone called the acromium (the bone you feel when you place your fingers on the top of your shoulder) and over a floor of bone called the humeral head (the top of your upper arm bone). Between these two bones is a small space through which your main rotator cuff muscle lives as it goes away from the neck and ends on the outside of your humerus. When you swim, the repetitive stroke action of your arms impinges or pinches this tendon between these two bones and causes tendonitis or even tearing. This is worse if the shoulder girdle is weak. Healing of this tendon is slow because it has a poor blood supply.

Keep your rotator cuff strong with the exercises in the Fit to Go section in Chapter 6, and avoid using hand paddles, which increase the upward pressure of the humeral head on the supraspinatus muscle.

Cycling

Cyclists get injured not only because of the terrible toos but also because equipment is so important to the overall kinetics of your ride. Here are a few things to keep in mind about your bike and riding in general:

- For a road bike, keep your frame size 2.5 cm from crotch to top-tube. For an off-road bike, keep it 7–15 cm.

- Seat height should allow approximately 30 degrees of knee bend at the lowest point. A low seat forces the knee to bend more and may cause knee pain.

- The forward tip of the saddle to the center of the handlebars should equal the distance from the tip of your elbow to your long finger. Although a longer crank length gives you a mechanical advantage, it also forces your hips and knees through a larger range of motion and increases your risk of injury.

- If you are still using toe clips, exchange them for bike shoes to keep the ball of your foot over the pedal axel. This also helps to avoid foot nerve compression injuries and numb toes.

An important way to avoid cycling injuries is to get your bike fitted to your body at a reputable bike shop. In this process, they take a variety of measurements, only one of which is the distance between your feet and your seat, and adjust each component of your bike so that it is more efficient for your body.

To avoid the other cycling pitfalls that cause knee injury, modify your training to restrict intensity when you are sore or injured, keep your cadence greater than 90, and limit hill workouts until your symptoms subside. Keep your quads, hamstrings, and calves flexible. If you have access to a therapist with electrical stimulation, you can use it to strengthen both types of muscle fibers (fast and slow twitch) and equalize your medial and lateral quad strength (usually, the medial or inside portion of the quads is weaker than the lateral or outside portions). Orthotics or wedges may compensate for foot pronation (flat feet). You should also avoid squats and lunges while you are injured.

Cyclists may develop Achilles tendonitis from the repetitive dorsiflexion (ankle flexed up) during the power phase of cycling or if the seat is too low. If your foot does not flex up enough or is flat, you are at a higher risk for plantar fasciitis (inflammation of the tight tissue on the bottom of your foot). Forefoot pain can be avoided by preventing excessive resistance (too much pressure) in a low cadence (slow pedal speed).

CAN I EXERCISE WHEN I'M SICK?

Moderate exercisers are known to spend about 50 percent fewer days sick than non-exercisers, but what do we do when we do get sick? Drink lots of fluid, get some rest, and eat chicken soup—just like your mother said.

- If you have a cold with a stuffy nose, cough, aches, and pains, you can get back on track with intense exercise when your symptoms resolve and you can breathe.

- Walking is good for you any time and will not make your cold worse.

- If you have severe flu, a fever, or severe fatigue, you should give yourself one to two weeks to recover and then start exercising slowly.

Arthritis: Oh, My Aching Joints

Stiffness, aching, grinding, swelling, outright pain—these are all symptoms of arthritis and can be a barrier to staying mobile as we age. The good news is that there are many ways to treat arthritis and get you back into the game.

The Arthritis Foundation reports that 21 million people in the United States have arthritis. What exactly is this common affliction associated with aging? Simply, it is the wear and tear of the cartilage that lines the end of your bones. Normally, cartilage is smooth, glistening, and white, and two cartilage-covered bones moving across one another in our joints are virtually frictionless. In fact, they are smoother than ice. When the cartilage begins to wear down, like potholes in a road, the surface loses its smooth finish. This is when the stiffness and aching set in.

Recently, ThermaCare® asked baby boomers about living with arthritis. Sixty-seven percent reported having weekly muscle or joint pain. Of those with pain, 69 percent said they simply worked through the pain to remain active; 90 percent believed their pain was treatable and were looking for new and better ways to treat it.

If you have arthritis, this is a marvelous time to have it. What I mean by this is that there is virtually a smorgasbord of treatments to try while remaining active. Some of them are listed below.

Arthritis Home Remedies

Most people with arthritis experience a gradual onset of aches and pains in their joints and don't immediately make their way to a doctor's office. Here are some home therapies to try:

- *Heat therapy.* Warmth feels great on stiff joints in the morning when you wake up, before exercise, or while you are sitting in one place for a long time (like at work) and are creaky when you get up. The easiest way to apply heat is with one of the several available arthritis heat wraps. These disposable wraps warm up to 104°F, are air-activated, and last between eight and 12 hours. The warmth increases the blood supply to the joint and helps you move it through a range of motion. I like ThermaCare Arthritis HeatWraps® since they conform to the joint and last 12 hours. You can also use a heating pad, a moist towel warmed in the microwave (be careful not to burn yourself), or a hot water bottle. I do not recommend the variety of arthritis creams and gels that make the skin feel warm. Generally, they do not change the temperature of the actual soft tissues surrounding the joints, plus they leave you smelling medicated.

- *Ice therapy.* Ice is an excellent remedy after activity, at the end of a long day, or any time your joints ache. You should apply a bag of ice or a cold pack after exercise or any time a joint feels painful. Not only does this simple solution calm the inflammatory process going on in your knees but it confuses the pain pathways and decreases pain. A minimum of 20 to 30 minutes is necessary. Apply the ice pack or simply a bag filled with ice and wrapped in a thin towel over your joint. Our skin gets thinner with age, and the towel prevents damage. Generally, you should use ice after activity and reserve heat for warming up and getting going in the morning.

- *NSAIDs.* Most of you will say that you are not "pill people," but this class of drugs does not simply mask the pain— it actually treats the source. Non-steroidal anti-inflammatory drugs (e.g., ibuprofen, naprosyn, etodolac, celecoxib) are a class of medications that work directly at the cellular level to halt inflammation. In arthritis, you experience pain because of the toxins released from the inflammation of an arthritic joint. One purpose of this body reaction to injury is to clear away the cellular debris that happens with injury. The substances made by the body are powerful; I often describe what is going on in an inflamed joint as "chemical warfare." These toxins then inflame the tissue surrounding them and a circular pattern of pain and inflammation arises. You must nip the cycle in the bud and get rid of the toxins.

I would not suggest taking NSAIDs if they really did not make a huge impact on your discomfort. Taking them for arthritis is not like taking an aspirin for a headache. NSAIDs are most effective if taken regularly over a course of days. They are usually taken several times a day, and it takes several days to build up a therapeutic level in your blood. NSAIDs can have some side effects. They can increase your blood pressure or upset your stomach. Ask your doctor if taking NSAIDs is all right for you. This is especially important if you have stomach problems.

- *F.A.C.E.* You thought F.A.C.E.-ing your future was related only to how to exercise, didn't you? Every patient who comes to my office with arthritis pain is put on a flexibility, exercise, resistance, and balance program. I usually begin by sending them for six weeks to physical therapy to jump-start their program, and then they transition to a fitness program if they are not already on one.

Keeping your joints supple by stretching is important since arthritis tends to make joints even stiffer than what would occur in one's body due to the effects of aging alone. Aerobic exercise is key for maintaining overall musculoskeletal health. With arthritis, you may need to modify what you do to keep active. For instance, swim in a warm pool, cycle, or spin to take the load off your leg joints; use the elliptical machine instead of running. The fitness component is also important in maintaining a healthy body weight. Excess weight is felt by your joints! Did you know that your knees bear five to seven times your body weight with every step? This means that for every extra 10 pounds you weigh, your knees feel like they are carrying 70 extra pounds. Stated positively, if you can lose the extra 10 pounds you are carrying around, your knees effectively lose 70!

If you have arthritis, it is vital that the muscles surrounding your joints become and remain strong in order to absorb some of the impact of daily activity. The key to your knees being able to handle this stress is the strength of your quadriceps. As every one of my patients can recite for you, "The quads are the key to the knees!" These four giant muscles on the front of your thighs can significantly assist your knees in bearing the load of your body if they are strong and decrease the pounding and pain your joints feel.

- *Balance and fall prevention*. You must retrain your muscles and muscle/brain pathways to maintain balance. As discussed in Chapter 7, as we age, we lose our ability to balance well, and arthritis makes this worse. Not only does our balance decrease in the knee with arthritis but it also decreases in the opposite knee. We don't know exactly why this occurs; we simply know that it does and adds up to a double whammy.

- *Active rest*. Finally, if you have pounded out an intense workout and your joints are sore, rest them. This does not mean sitting on the couch for several days. Instead, get on a bike and spin, row, use the elliptical, or work out your upper body alone one day. Rest is great . . . when it is active.

In our survey of 2001 Senior Olympians, there was a definite association between having arthritis and injury. People with arthritis were twice as likely to have five musculoskeletal injuries and three times more likely to have injuries around the knees. This is because of quadriceps weakness and altered balance. The physical therapy prescription for my patients with arthritis therefore reads:

- Heat/cold therapy

- Joint range of motion

- Strengthening of quadriceps, core, and hips

- A fitness program transitioning to a home program

- Balance and equilibrium training

Arthritis Remedies from Your Doctor

- *Joint injections.* There are two categories of joint injections physicians use to relieve arthritis pain: steroid injections and joint lubrication. Steroid injections have been around for a long time and consist of injecting the joint with a mixture of numbing medicine, such as lidocaine or marcaine, and steroids. The point of this injection is to decrease the pain and inflammation of arthritis. These injections usually last an average of three weeks, and most physicians will give only three a year to any joint. I tend not to use steroids unless my patients have excruciating pain. I prefer to use joint lubrication with a class of injection called hyaluronic acid. (There are currently five of these on the market. Four are purified from the comb of roosters, and the fifth is grown in bacteria and then purified for injection.) The hyaluronic acid works to decrease inflammation and lubricate the joint. It causes the joint lining to secrete substances that feed the remaining cartilage. Hyaluronic acid injections work best in early arthritis and can be effective up to six months or longer. They are given once a week for three to five weeks and can be repeated every six months if patients receive significant relief.

Last week, I began the fourth round of hyaluronic acid injections into the left knee of one of my patients named Mark. A 54-year-old insurance salesman, he always hurries in between his business appointments for his knee injections. Mark lays down on the exam table and pulls up his trouser leg, I inject his knee and he runs out the door to his next meeting. Not much inconvenience for the six months of pain relief and the increased function he gets.

When he was in high school, Mark had some kind of knee injury, and now his left knee has significant arthritis with narrowing of the joint space and bone spurs, called osteophytes, around the bone edges. This arthritis caused his knee to ache day and night and had begun to limit his activity. Worse yet, Mark began to gain weight from being more sedentary. Today, his right knee is completely normal, with wide-open joint spaces and no pain, but his left knee needs help. When he first came to me and I diagnosed where his pain was coming from, he was a little skeptical of my three-prong regimen of NSAIDs, physical fitness, and hyaluronic acid injections. After I made my case for why these three approaches are key, he agreed to try them. Well, two years later and starting his fourth round of biannual injections, Mark is a true believer in this method. For Mark and many of my other patients, arthritis does not mean the end of their active lives. It simply means we have to harness all the treatments available to keep them going.

- *Joint bracing*. Knee arthritis can cause legs, in particular, to move from straight to bowlegged or knock-kneed. This is because as one side of the knee wears down, the joint on that side collapses. Most people wear down the inside compartment of the knee first and end up with bowlegs. Braces can "unload" the affected side of the joint by pushing on the opposite side and effectively straightening the leg again. For instance, if you have arthritis on the inside side of your knee and develop bowlegs, the brace will unload that side by pushing against the outside side of the knee. The problem with knee braces is that they work only if they are worn daily, and many people simply put them in the closet. These braces are custom braces made especially for you and must be ordered by your physician. The stretchy knee sleeves you can buy in the pharmacy are not effective in unloading the knee and are not what I am describing here. Some of my patients like the sleeves, though, because they make them more aware of their knees and they feel more stable. A study found that for decreasing knee pain and increasing stability, the braces were the best and the sleeves were better than nothing.

•   *Alternative/complementary therapies.* Many patients ask me if using herbs or alternative therapies will help their arthritis. Although many people swear by products such as chondroitin sulfate, glucosamine, and shark cartilage, there is currently no convincing evidence in the medical literature that these remedies are better than a sugar pill. A recent study, however, shows that acupuncture can relieve arthritis pain. To this end, I tell my patients that as long as the alternative therapy is not hurting them—and they think it is possibly helping—then they are welcome to take it.

•   *Arthroscopic joint debridement.* "Washing the joint out" by surgically removing loose tissue or debris in the joint using a small camera and instruments inserted through tiny incisions has not been found to be effective for long-term treatment of arthritis pain. The only true indication for arthroscopic surgery with arthritis is if the person has mechanical catching or locking (which feels like popping, snapping, or sharp pain) because of a torn meniscus. The meniscus is the wedge-like rubbery cushion located between the femur (thighbone) and tibia (shinbone) and is responsible for supporting 80 percent of the body's weight. It thus protects the ends of the bones from grinding on each other. The menisci (you have two in each knee) are among the most commonly injured parts of the knee. They are separate from the cartilage that coats the ends of the bones. If you want to think about the knee in layers going from the thighbone to the shinbone, each side would go: thighbone, cartilage, meniscus, cartilage, shinbone.

If you play a contact or noncontact sport, you may tear the meniscus by twisting the knee, pivoting, cutting, or decelerating. You can injure your meniscus without any trauma since the collagen weakens and wears thin over time, setting the stage for a degenerative tear. Arthroscopic surgery is useful if loose bodies (pieces of cartilage or bone that break off) are getting caught in the joint. The surgery will eliminate the mechanical symptoms but will not touch the aching pain of arthritis. I always make this distinction clear to my patients.

My Arthritis Protocol

After I examine my patients and go over their X-rays with them, we discuss their arthritis and the treatments available. I initially treat them using the following three-pronged approach:

1. NSAIDs to decrease inflammation and pain
2. Physical therapy with a transition to a fitness program to work on range of motion, strength, balance, and weight control
3. Injections by hyaluronic acid to lubricate and feed the remaining cartilage

Every athlete at some point experiences injury. As a mature athlete or adult onset exerciser, injury and arthritis may be a part of your challenge to stay active. Your goal should be to prevent those repetitive injuries that sideline your future and listen to your body when it tells you it is hurting so you can treat it actively.

HOME**WORK**

Have you ever been injured doing sports? What were you doing? Did you have a case of the terrible toos, or was your injury a sudden traumatic event? Do you get the same or similar injuries over and over again? If the answers to these questions are *yes*, then try to think about the factors leading to these injuries and how they can be prevented. Was it simply a matter of repetitive motion, or are there skills you need to learn in order to prevent future setbacks?

"If it weren't for the fact that the TV set and the refrigerator are so far apart, some of us wouldn't get any exercise at all."

—Joey Adams (1911–1999), U.S. comedian, nightclub performer, and columnist for the *New York Post*

Healing with Steel

When the pain and functional disability of arthritis are causing a daily decline in the quality of life of one of my patients, we discuss total joint replacement. Many people cringe when they hear those words. However, we are talking about replacing parts of your body that no longer serve you with parts that will. It may be a little hard to grasp when you first think about it, but we want to make you a little "bionic," like the Six Million Dollar Man.

Today, doctors are capable of replacing many joints in the body, from your knuckles to your ankles, but the knees and hips are the most commonly replaced joints. The American Academy of Orthopaedic Surgeons estimates that between now and the year 2030, there will be a 673 percent increase in the number of total knee replacements and a 174 percent increase in the number of total hip replacements performed. The increases will be the result of the aging of our population and improvements in joint technology.

I was taught and I teach my residents that "we don't treat X-rays no matter what they look like; we treat the patients." This means that we don't replace a joint just because a person's X-ray shows a lot of arthritis. We replace joints only when patients have a high grade of arthritis and have tried conservative measures and they say either, "Doc, I can't take the pain another day," or, "Doc, you have got to help me get my life back." Then we are ready to discuss joint replacement.

CONSIDERING JOINT REPLACEMENT

There are many issues to consider when deciding to undergo joint replacement. Traditionally, doctors waited until patients were as old as possible before replacing their joints because the average total joint will last only between 10 and 15 years. At that point, many joints require revision surgery to replace worn parts. For patients, waiting until some arbitrary old age to have a joint replaced means suffering with the pain and debilitation of arthritis, cutting back their activity, becoming sedentary, and in many instances needing to take chronic pain medications—all the while waiting until the magic year when a surgeon finally decides they were old enough.

Today, there is a trend to replace worn-out joints earlier in order to give the person another 10 to 15 years of active life. Yes, this means that some people will require additional surgery for joint revision at some point, but it also means that instead of sitting around getting fat and debilitated, many people can resume or increase the activity in their lives. In addition, improved joint technology and new joint materials are making it possible for joints to last longer, so revision surgery might not be necessary for more than 15 years.

I have a patient named Larry. He is a giant man towering more than 6 feet 5 inches and once weighing almost 500 pounds. Larry had been an athlete in high school and college, and after graduating, he kept consuming the calories of a high-level athlete even though he stopped exercising like one. The weight eventually added up. Larry remained as active as he could and coached his son's football team until he just couldn't take the pain in his knees anymore. His weight and natural anatomy had destroyed the cartilage in his knees, and he was walking around with bones grinding on bones like a mortar and pestle. At only 36 years old, Larry was no longer able to play with his five children and was beginning to have difficulty holding down his job.

Traveling from doctor to doctor looking for an answer to his debilitating knee pain, Larry was told repeatedly that he was too overweight and too young for knee replacements. He was determined to get his life back, however, and over the course of a year lost nearly 200 pounds. However, his knees were still not participating in his life and were still causing him pain. When he finally came to see me, he was still young and a giant, but he had done the hard work of losing almost half his body weight. He was frustrated and almost in tears as I too expressed to him my concern about replacing his knees because of his young age.

As a surgeon, I had a decision to make. Did I sentence this young man to 15 more years of pain, disability, and certain sedentary lifestyle by saying no to replacing his knees, or did I bite the bullet and give this man a license for mobility by replacing his arthritic knees with new ones made of cobalt-chrome? Both Larry and I knew he would certainly require revision surgery some time in the future. But because my goal is to keep people as mobile as possible for as long as possible and prevent the ravages of Sedentary Death Syndrome, I replaced his right knee last year.

Larry flew through the three months of rehab without a hitch, and even at his first post-op visit, he came in beaming from ear to the ear. The only pain left in his right knee was the incision pain: The grinding pain that had taken away his active life was gone. Over the course of the next year, Larry returned to work, began coaching his son's team again, and loved his new lease on mobility. Last month, I replaced his other knee. Yesterday, I was walking through our physical therapy gym and there was Larry, riding a stationary bike, working up a sweat, beaming from ear to ear, and asking me to send him back to work. New knees gave life back to this young man so that he can again enjoy his children, wife, and job.

Joint replacements are meant to eliminate pain, restore limb alignment, and restore function. Many people think that having such operations means giving up an active lifestyle. In fact, the opposite is true. I want and expect patients to get moving after I replace their knees and hips, and I allow them to do anything they want except run. Running within a sport, such as tennis, is all right, but putting in 20 or 30 or more miles per week on the road is not the best for maintaining your new joints.

WILL A NEW JOINT GIVE YOU YOUR OLD LIFE BACK?

"I've got to be back on my feet by April so I can train for the drum and bugle corps world championships this summer. I have not missed a competition in 20 years and if we win we will be four-time world champs." I did not know that adults competed in drum and bugle corps competitions or how serious these events were, but my patient George was eager to teach me. This 54-year-old marcher had torn his ACL (anterior cruciate ligament) as a youth and never had it fixed. Now he had end-stage arthritis on the inside of his knee, and it was preventing him from marching at 80–90 steps per minute for hours on end. On top of that, the pain was so great that he could hardly function the day after he worked out. I could tell by talking to George that suggesting an alternative means of exercising was not going to fly. We had six months until the competition, and it usually takes three months to rehab back to sports after a total knee replacement. We had no time to waste.

George worked really hard in therapy, beginning the day after his operation. He walked the hallways of the hospital and kept his eye on the prize as he pushed himself back to full activity. Ultimately, he was able to march at a cadence of 80–90 steps per minute all while playing a bugle. I recently received a picture in the mail of George wearing his blue and white competition uniform with the gold medal of victory around his neck. For George, knee replacement was a license for mobility that gave him his life back.

HOW IS JOINT REPLACEMENT DONE?

When cartilage wears down and the bones begin to rub on one another, it causes both pain and deformity. One side of the knee wears out faster than the other, and the bones become lopsided. Most people wear out the inside (medial) portion of the knee joint and the top of the hip joint first. This is why you see many people becoming bowlegged as they age.

All joint replacements, therefore, are meant to decrease pain and realign joints so that they are straight again. Joint replacement is performed by making an incision over the involved joint and removing the ends of the bones that no longer have cartilage on them. Special jigs are used to measure and align the cuts made on the ends of the bones to make sure the new joint is anatomically aligned like the natural joint was before arthritis wore it down. Today, doctors are even using computer navigation in the operating room to more precisely align the bone cuts back to their natural anatomic position. Once all the bone cuts have been made, the ends of the bones are replaced with metal replicas. Prior to surgery, X-rays are measured to make sure that the proper sized implants are available, and during surgery, the surgeon measures to determine what size joint replacement is needed. When the surgeon confirms the proper size and alignment of the implants, they are cemented into place. This is why you can walk on joint replacements immediately.

The implants are made out of cobalt-chrome, ceramic, or titanium alloys and are polished to a highly shiny surface. They reflect light like a polished chrome bumper or a mirror. Between the two polished steel implants, a very tough piece of plastic, called polyethylene or poly, is inserted. The two bone ends move over this poly surface like your natural joint moved over its cartilage.

Rehabilitation after joint replacement surgery can take three to six months depending on the kind of shape a patient is in prior to surgery. The postoperative results are generally excellent with significant relief of pain and return of function. More than 90 percent of people continue to have good or excellent results more than 10 years after joint replacement. You can find more information about

METAL MEETS THE ROAD

It's interesting to note that here in Pittsburgh, many of the Senior Olympians who participated in the 2005 games had previous joint replacements. Even some of the cyclists had metal in their hips. While I encourage as much activity as possible from my patients with total joint replacements, some sports are better than others once you are bionic. Here are some of the preferred games for people with replacement hips and knees.

Total knee replacement

- Aerobics
- Cycling
- Dancing
- Golf
- Horseback riding
- Skiing
- Walking
- Swimming
- Tennis

Total hip replacement

- Aerobics
- Cycling
- Dancing
- Golf
- Swimming
- Tennis
- Walking

joint replacement at the American Academy of Orthopaedic Surgeons website at *orthoinfo.aaos.org/menus/arthroplasty.cfm*.

If you are thinking about having a total joint replacement, the most important word for you right now is *Pre-hab*. This means getting in as good shape as you possibly can *before* you have your surgery. This will enable you to recover and get out of the hospital faster, perform your exercises better after surgery, and ultimately get back to life sooner. A good place to start getting in shape for joint replacement is with the leg and core exercises you have already learned.

HOME**WORK**

If you have been told that you need a joint replacement, you have homework to do before you sign up. Find the answers to these questions:

- *How many joint replacements does your surgeon do a year?* You want to find a surgeon whose practice is primarily joint replacement.

- *Does your surgeon do her own revision/complication surgery, or does she refer this out?* You want a surgeon who not only performs the primary surgery but will also continue to care for you over the years if you have problems.

- *Will your surgeon send you for Pre-hab before surgery?* If your insurance pays for it or if you are willing to invest in this yourself, Pre-hab will make a big difference in how strong you feel when you recover.

- *How many days will you be in the hospital?* The typical hospital stay for a knee replacement is three to five days. For a hip replacement, it is one to three days.

- *Will you have inpatient or outpatient rehabilitation after surgery?* For both knee and hip replacements, after you leave the hospital, you may go to an inpatient rehabilitation center for a week or so of intensive physical rehab. If you go straight home from the hospital, you will immediately begin therapy as an outpatient.

- *What kind of blood thinner will you use? Shots or pills?* After a knee or hip replacement, it is standard practice to take a blood thinner to prevent blood clots in the legs. Blood clots are not common but can cause problems if they occur. Blood thinners, in the form of shots or pills, are typically given for three weeks after surgery.

"Today, the most common form of physical ABUSE is DISUSE."

—**Stephen Seiler, Ph.D.,**
Institute of Public Health, Sport,
and Nutrition, University of Agder,
Kristiansand, Norway

It's a Waistline, Not a Wasteline

The Fuel and Fluid of Peak Performance

So far, we have talked about how our bodies change with age, how to strategically plan to F.A.C.E. your exercise future, and how to prevent and treat injuries. Now we need to talk about how you are going to fuel the revolution that will be taking place in your body. I suspect that if you have given little thought to investing in your mobility, you have also not spent a lot of time being strategic about how you fuel your body. I have to admit that this is probably the area I am worst in myself.

171

While in training, young surgeons never know when they are going to have a minute to eat or sleep or go to the bathroom again, so we eat whatever we have access to whenever we have access to it (because the next time may not be until tomorrow). Sometimes it feels like a matter of survival just to grab whatever old, stale, fatty meal or candy bar is around. When I was an intern (when you are the lowest on the totem pole, in the most hectic year in training) and working 120 hours per week (this was before the current 80-hour workweek), I would even go as far as consoling myself over having to be running around the hospital and trauma bay in the middle of the night by sneaking up to the cafeteria at 2 A.M. for a cheeseburger and fries. I deserved it, right? Seven years of this unplanned survival-type eating resulted in my slowly gaining 25 pounds. It wasn't that I was sedentary—I was running around the hospital 120 hours each week and ran a marathon—it was just that I was putting trash in and getting trash out.

You don't have to be a surgical intern to run around all week not thinking about what you are putting into your body. It is too easy for all of us to curb our afternoon cravings at the vending machine. If you are putting trash in, you too will get trash out.

The rest of this chapter outlines what our bodies need as fuel. For some of you, this will be new information; for others, it is perhaps a quick review. But this chapter is not a diet plan. If you want one, there are thousands of books about dieting. I do not advocate dieting or being austere with yourself. I think this just makes you obsess even more about what food you are not getting to eat. Instead, I advocate knowing what your body needs and being smart about what you eat. I will never tell you not to taste that chocolate cake. I will simply tell you not to eat it all the time.

ENERGY REQUIREMENTS: PLAYING THE NUMBERS

When was the last time you weighed what you were supposed to? High school? When you got married? Last summer? Can't remember? No matter how long ago it was, gaining and losing weight is not a complicated or mystical goal that few can grasp. It is a numbers game. Unless you have a real medical problem such as thyroid dysfunction or diabetes, to lose weight, you just have to take in fewer calories than you expend. Did I hear the crowd say "Duh?" It sounds simple, and it is, yet more than two-thirds of us don't have a handle on how to consume only what we need each day. In fact, I think that weight gain and getting out of shape can be such a gradual process that we don't realize it is happening until 10 or 20 pounds later.

When sedentary people begin one of my exercise programs, I have their body composition measured. We are able to tell exactly what percentage of their body is lean and what percentage is fat. In my last session of 89 sedentary people beginning to exercise, the average body fat for the women was 51 percent and for the men, 41 percent. In contrast, a healthy body fat is 18–25 percent. The people whose body fat we measured looked like average citizens you see on the street. They knew they had a few pounds to lose but would never have guessed how much extra weight they were carrying around. They were surprised and taken aback by their bodies. In short, it is easy not to notice what is happening to you.

The first step in beating the numbers is being aware of what you are taking in. For instance, if you go out and walk or run three miles, you burn approximately 300 calories. If you then go out and reward yourself with a creamy, frothy, iced coffee drink, you pour 600 calories back in and you need to go out and do another three miles just to break even. Start reading the labels of the foods you eat. Notice what the manufacturer considers a serving size (often much less than we actually eat) and how many calories that amount contains. I think you will surprised by how quickly the calories add up.

When you are out at a typical restaurant (where the serving sizes are like small platters), try to divide everything except the veggies in half and eat only one of those halves. I know this goes against the "clean your plate" and "children in Ethiopia" mantras that we have heard all our lives, but do it anyway. In addition, if you start dinner by drinking a glass of water and then eat slowly, you will feel full and still enjoy the delicious flavors. I promise that anyone living in the United States today is unlikely to starve by eating only half of what is presented to her. (Besides, you can take the part you didn't eat home to have for lunch the next day.)

A POUND A WEEK

Healthy, sustainable weight loss is approximately one pound per week. This means burning 500 calories more than you take in each day. When you think about it, that is not really too much sacrifice. It means cutting out the morning Danish, not drinking two cans of soda while on break, or walking past the candy machine. Are you saying "blah, blah, blah, we have heard this before"? You probably have, and yet you may not be in control of your intake. I have to control mine. I love sweets, so I have to make a conscious decision every time I pass the vending machines at work. After I am good for several days and don't stop for an afternoon candy bar, I have to have a talk with myself: "Vonda, you went two days without that Snickers bar and didn't shrivel up and die. Walk on by." After a while, I get to the point where I don't want to break my streak of good behavior.

On the other hand, if you want to lose a pound a week but don't want to limit your intake, you can eat what you normally do and run five miles a day (burning 500 calories). I know one pound doesn't seem like a lot, but it is a start. And truthfully, if you ramp up your exercise and watch what you eat at the same time, you are likely to lose more than that. When I finished my surgical training and had more control of my time, I stopped the 2 A.M. consolation meal, avoided the "eat whenever you can" tactic, and ramped up my running. I spent more energy than I took in, and the weight fell off.

As a quick aside, if you are a woman in your 40s who thinks her metabolism (the way we turn food into energy) has really slowed down since your 30s, I urge you to get your weight under control before you hit menopause and your metabolism slows down even more. It only gets harder then.

DETERMINING YOUR ENERGY NEEDS

The medical literature is full of studies that recognize the importance of proper nutrition for exercise performance. What you put in your body affects not only your overall health and weight but your recovery time and performance. Athletes of any level, independent of age, must consume adequate dietary energy to offset energy expenditure, maintain body weight and health, and maximize training effort. Too much in and you get fat. Too little in and you get muscle and bone loss (the body uses itself as a resource/storehouse), increased fatigue, injury, and illness. But how much is enough?

There is a classic equation for predicting how much energy you need just to survive, or your basal metabolic rate (BMR). It is called the Harris Benedict Equation and uses sex, weight, height, and age to predict your energy requirements.

Women: **BMR = 655 + (4.35 × weight in pounds) + (4.7 × height in inches) – (4.7 × age in years)**

Men: **BMR = 66 + (6.23 × weight in pounds) + (12.7 × height in inches) – (6.8 × age in years)**

For example, for a 40-year-old woman who is 64 inches tall and weighs 116 pounds:

BMR = 655 + (4.35 × 116 pounds) + (4.7 × 64 inches) – (4.7 × 40 years) = 1272.4

Then, to determine your total calorie needs to maintain your current weight, multiply your BMR by your activity factor:

Sedentary (little or no exercise): **BMR × 1.2 = daily calorie needs**

Lightly active (light exercise one to three times a week): **BMR × 1.375 = daily calorie needs**

Moderately active (moderate exercise three to five times a week): **BMR × 1.55 = daily calorie needs**

Very active (hard exercise six to seven times a week): **BMR × 1.725 = daily calorie needs**

Extra active (very hard exercise/sports/physical job): **BMR × 1.9 = daily calorie needs**

For example, for a 40-year-old woman who is 64 inches tall, weighs 116 pounds, and does five days of moderate exercise per week:

**BMR × 1.55 = 1272.4 × 1.55 = 1972.2 calories a day
to maintain her current weight**

If she were a couch potato, the same woman could only eat 1526.8 calories per day without gaining weight.

This formula is good for most people but underestimates the energy needs of a highly muscular person since muscle burns more energy just for cells to function without doing any extra activity. The formula also overestimates the calories of a fat person since fat burns less energy for normal metabolism.

Now you have a number to keep in the front of your mind. To become aware of what you are taking in, read the labels of the foods you eat for a week and write the calories down. This is just like keeping track of what comes in and what goes out of your checkbook. If it seems like the number you calculated is too high and you are taking in less energy than the formula predicted and still gaining weight, it may be that your body composition does not require that many calories to maintain or that your metabolism is very slow. Kicking up your metabolism with exercise or building muscle will help.

A recent study in the *Journal of the American Medical Association* found that for overall health, fitness was more important than fatness. This means that even if you are carrying a few extra pounds, taking the steps to get fit will benefit your overall health more than losing weight but remaining sedentary. That's why diets alone are not as good as watching what you eat while getting fit.

Research has shown that when you initially go from sedentary to active, you do not experience significantly higher dietary energy requirements during the first few months of aerobic or resistance training. By initiating a program with the four F.A.C.E. components, you will therefore use more energy than

OF PEARS AND APPLES

Where you carry your extra weight is as important as how much you are carrying. You are either a *pear* who carries your extra weight around your hips or an *apple* who carries your extra weight around your waist. It is better to be a pear than an apple. Those of you who inherited apple-shaped bodies, with weight carried at the waistline, are at increased risk for overall health problems such as diabetes, heart disease, high blood pressure, and obesity. You were born this way, but you can decrease your health risk by minimizing your fat storage through activity. As long as you avoid excess weight, being an apple or a pear doesn't put you at special risk.

If you are sitting there shaking your head doubting this whole fruity business, I don't blame you. But this is serious stuff. If you are an apple, raise your hand. According to Dr. Paul Ribisl, the former chair of the Department of Health and Exercise Science at Wake Forest University, apple-shaped people spend more on healthcare and medication than smokers or alcoholics and are most at risk for developing diabetes, high cholesterol, metabolic syndrome, and all the morbid consequences of these diseases.

you take in. The more fat you burn as energy, the leaner you will be. This works in your favor since muscle burns more energy just to live than fat does, as discussed above. Pound for pound, the leaner you are, the more energy you burn.

Physicians traditionally used body mass index (BMI) as a way to assess a person's risk for disease. The problem with this measurement alone is that it does not account for the very lean person who weighs more per inch than a fat person since muscle weighs more than fat. A more accurate way to determine health risk is to combine your BMI measurement with your waist circumference measurement (remember, it matters where the fat is stored). Ideally, men's waists should be less than 40 inches and women's less than 35.

The National Institutes of Health outlines the risk of developing severe health problems according to body mass index (BMI) and waist circumference. Review Table 1 and see where you stand. If you fall in one of the obese categories, now is the time to put feet to your desire to change your health. I suggest seeing your doctor, checking out your local hospital's wellness programs for personal assistance, or even coming to the University of Pittsburgh's weight management and wellness programs. I would be happy to set you up with our experts.

MACRONUTRIENTS: CARBOHYDRATES, PROTEINS, FATS, AND FLUIDS

Muscles get energy to propel you along by tapping into your muscle glycogen (the form of carbohydrates in which carbohydrates are stored). When these are diminished, you start to depend on

Table 1. The Risk of Developing Health Problems According to Body Mass Index and Waist Circumference

Rating	BMI	Obesity class	Men: Waist < 40 in. Women: Waist < 35 in.	Men: Waist < 40 in. Women: Waist < 35 in.
Underweight	< 18.5	—	—	—
Normal	18.5–24.9	—	—	Central obesity is a health risk
Overweight	25–29.9	—	Increased	High
Obese	30–34.9	I	High	Very High
	35–39.9	II	Very High	Very High
Extreme	> 40	III	Extremely High	Extremely High

your blood glucose to keep going. Blood glucose is derived from carbohydrates, fat, and protein. If you can't maintain your blood sugar levels, your performance will flounder.

Carbohydrates are the largest contributor to the energy pool. Fat contributes to your energy pool over a wide range of exercise intensities but decreases as you exercise harder because carbs will contribute more. Proteins contribute less than 5 percent of energy used during exercise but contribute to your overall pool during rest. The exception to this is during endurance exercise, when your liver begins to synthesize energy from protein.

The American Dietetic Association (ADA) and the Food and Nutrition Board of the Institute of Medicine at the National Academy of Sciences list the energy requirements for older athletes as 55–58 percent from carbohydrates, 12–15 percent from protein, and 25–30 percent from fat. If you are a high-level athlete with frequent intense workouts, you should seek one-on-one advice from a sports nutritionist to work out a plan to optimize your nutrition because you may need more protein for increased workouts.

Carbohydrates

Contrary to popular diets, carbohydrates (carbs) are not the enemy. The cells of your body use circulating glucose to make energy at rest and during exercise. Not only do your cells need carbohydrates but your brain is entirely dependent on carbs for energy. Carbs help maintain blood glucose during exercise and restore muscle glycogen during rest and recovery from exercise. The recommended intake is a minimum of 130 grams/day, or 45–65 percent of daily calories for adults, independent of age or activity level. This is the minimum needed for your brain to function. Athletes are recommended to consume 6–10 grams for every kilogram of body weight per day. For example, a typical man weighing 70 kilograms needs 420 grams of carbs per day to fuel his activity. If you are on a low-calorie diet (less than 2000 calories per day), it may be difficult to achieve the 6 grams per day.

Age does not alter the role of carbs in generating energy, and older athletes continue to be able to store ingested carbs as glycogen in the liver and muscle tissue, using the glycogen as a source of energy-producing material during exercise. For exercise lasting an hour or more, eating 30 to 60 grams of carbs, as either food or beverage, is recommended. This is the purpose of all those nutrition bars and gel packs. (Try them out at home before you hit the road or gym with them because they can sometimes cause stomach upset or diarrhea.)

After hard exercise (lasting more than 90 minutes), recovery is optimal if you eat some carbs after exercise. This should consist of 1.5 grams of carbs per kilogram of body weight. An additional carb feeding two hours later will help restore muscle glycogen storage. These recommendations are for aging athletes who train hard and frequently. If you are a recreational athlete and do a race every once in a while, you do not have to worry about recovering with carbs.

Protein

The predominant role of protein for exercise is to repair the microdamage that occurs to muscle and bone. Protein also supports immune function. A small amount—about 5 percent—is used to fuel exercise. The Recommended Daily Allowance (RDA) of protein is 0.8 grams per kilogram of weight per day for the average person (an ounce of fish or meat has approximately 7 grams of protein).

The ADA concludes that highly physically active male endurance athletes require a maximum of 1.2 to 1.4 grams per kilogram of weight per day; and strength training requires 1.6 to

FOODS HIGH IN PROTEIN

Beef

- 7 grams of protein per ounce

Chicken

- Breast: 30 grams per 3.5 ounces
- Thigh: 10 grams per ounce
- Drumstick: 11 grams per ounce
- Wing: 6 grams per ounce

Fish

- 22 grams per 3.5 ounces

Pork

- Chop: 22 grams per 3 ounces
- Ham: 19 grams per 3 ounces
- Bacon (1 slice): 3 grams

Ostrich

- 10 grams per ounce

Eggs/Dairy

- Large egg: 6 grams
- Milk (1 cup): 8 grams
- Yogurt (1 cup): 8–12 grams

Beans/Nuts

- Most beans: 7–10 grams per ½ cup

- Peanut butter (2 tablespoons): 8 grams

- Almonds (¼ cup): 8 grams

- Peanuts (¼ cup): 9 grams

- Pumpkin seeds (¼ cup): 19 grams

1.7 grams per kilogram of weight per day to accumulate and maintain muscles. This higher requirement is needed to provide amino acids, or protein building blocks, for the repair of exercise-induced muscle damage, the buildup of lean tissue mass, and the use of protein as an energy source during exercise. (Note that there are no data for women.) Eating a high-protein diet or taking supplements that provide more than these levels is unlikely to increase muscle mass further.

Although any flip through an exercise magazine will leave you inundated with protein supplement ads, the data on taking amino acid supplements is inconclusive. For most people, adequate protein can be obtained by eating complete sources of protein such as dairy, meats, eggs, and fish.

There are no specific recommendations for older athletes or older sedentary people, for that matter. Several studies do show that the Recommended Daily Allowance for protein may not be adequate for sustaining and building muscle for aging athletes. If you exercise or weight train without enough protein intake, your body will use itself—your own muscles—as a protein source, and you will have muscle atrophy and loss of fat-free body mass.

Leaders in nutrition recommend that masters athletes take in the 1.2 to 1.4 grams per kilogram of weight per day of protein.

You can get this amount from milk, eggs, cheese, yogurt, lean meat, fish, and poultry. You do not need to buy buckets of protein powder at the health food store. A word of caution: This recommendation is for healthy people, not those with chronic diseases that require therapeutic diets.

Eating protein with every meal, even breakfast, will make you feel full longer, and may keep you from snacking. This can be as simple as eating a handful of almonds.

Fats

Fat is not all bad. Despite its bad rap, it provides energy for exercise, and is the essential element of cell membranes. Fat also provides vitamins E, A, and D. There is no RDA for total fat, but a daily energy intake with 20–35 percent of energy from fat will provide adequate energy while preventing the risk of chronic disease from too high fat intake. The American College of Sports Medicine recommends that you get fat energy from 10 percent saturated fats, 10 percent polyunsaturated fats, and 10 percent monounsaturated fats. Lower levels do not enhance physical performance.

Fluids

The adult body is 50–70 percent water. The leaner you are, the greater your percent water since muscle contains more than 80 percent water while fat has less than 30 percent. Disturbances in water and electrolyte balance affect us at all levels from systemic to cellular and prevent our ability to continue exercising.

Hot and dry will hurt you. Even modest dehydration (less than 2 percent fluid loss) can affect athletic performance. When you are dehydrated, you sweat at a slower rate and therefore cannot cool your body as effectively. Overheating impairs cardiovascular function and strains the heart. As you lose water, there is a linear rise in core body temperature with every one liter of water loss resulting in an increase of 0.3 degrees Celsius.

Age-related changes amplify this effect. With age, we have an altered thirst mechanism. Our kidneys can become less efficient, we waste more water, and our blood vessels are less flexible and dilate less. When this happens to our blood vessels, it reduces our ability to release heat through the skin.

Do not trust your thirst. Your thirst mechanism is not strong enough to stimulate adequate fluid intake during exercise. You must therefore have a fluid plan for optimal performance. This plan is divided into pre-hydration before exercise, hydration during exercise, and re-hydration after exercise.

Pre-Hydration

It is easier to prevent dehydration than to catch up during exercise. The American College of Sports Medicine recommends consuming 500 mL (about one average bottle of water) of fluid one to two hours prior to exercise to make sure you are ready to exercise and to give yourself time to get rid of the extra fluid.

Hydration

Hydration is meant to prevent or minimize dehydration during exercise. For exercise that lasts less than one hour, water is hydration enough. There is no evidence that you need carb drinks if you are going to exercise less than one hour. When exercising one hour or more, carbohydrate drinks should be taken. This will prevent the muscle fatigue that usually occurs with exercise lasting more than one hour. Carb drinks should have a 4–8 percent concentration since a concentration greater than 10 percent will cause fluid to be drawn into the gut (water always moves to the place where its concentration is lowest), which not only removes the fluid from your body's availability but could cause diarrhea.

Gastric emptying means how fast the fluid you drink is used. To maximize fluid usage, you should keep your stomach as full of water as tolerated without vomiting—usually about 500 cc, or one bottle. Also, room temperature water is more readily used by the body than ice cold water. Regular exercise does not appear to alter gastric emptying; high-intensity exercise at 80 percent or more of maximum inhibits gastric emptying. During exercise, sweat should be replaced by fluid intake of 6–12 ounces every 20 minutes. Begin drinking early during your exercise; it is better to prevent dehydration than play catch-up. This is easier said than done when you are focusing on exercise or a race. It is not uncommon for us to become so dehydrated that we lose 2–3 kilograms of body weight during a race from water loss alone.

The early signs of dehydration are subtle and may be easy to miss. They include dark yellow urine, dry mouth, headaches, weakness, irritability, and cramping. When dehydration progresses, you may not urinate or tear or may experience fainting, rapid heart rate, low blood pressure, and changes in clarity of thought.

Re-Hydration

After exercise, you will probably be thirsty. Even if you are not, drink anyway. It is common for us to dehydrate our body weight by 2–6 percent during exercise, especially in the heat. For every pound that you sweat off, you should drink 16–23 ounces after an exercise session. Avoid caffeine or alcohol (even if your race is sponsored by Bud Light). You will know that you have hydrated back up to normal when your urine is clear or pale. If it remains yellow or dark, drink up.

ARE YOU A SALTY SWEATER?

During my pre-performance physical of Mike, one of my PRIMA athletes, he mentioned that he often got a lot of cramps after a long workout despite the fact that he drank adequate fluids and ate bananas (the supposed cramp prevention food) like they were going out of style. After further questioning, he mentioned that at the end of a marathon or on a really hot day, his skin will feel like gritty sandpaper covered in salt. Mike is a salty sweater: He loses a lot of salt through his skin while sweating. Although many of us are of the mindset that we need to limit our salt intake to decrease our chances of high blood pressure, when we sweat like this, we can actually have too little salt in our bodies. This can lead to cramps. . . . even if you are eating bananas like they are going out of style (bananas give you potassium but not a lot of salt). Mike met with PRIMA's nutritionist, Leslie Bonci, and she evaluated his diet and fluid intake. She discovered that he was not taking in enough salt (sodium) to replace the salt he lost during exercise. This was leading to his frequent cramps. She recommended he add a little salt to his diet with pretzels, soy sauce, and Worcestershire sauce, and miraculously his cramps decreased. Leslie also recommends drinking sports drinks during long workouts to replace the electrolytes (salt, potassium, etc.) you lose.

HYDRATION RECOMMENDATIONS

The following recommendations on hydration are from the American College of Sports Medicine.

- Eat and drink a balanced and adequate diet in the 24 hours prior to an event, including the meal prior to exercise.

- Drink 17 ounces (one standard bottle of water) within the two hours prior to exercise to provide adequate hydration and give you time to urinate the excess (nothing kills a workout—or worse, a race—than having to stop to use the bathroom).

- During a race, you should begin drinking early and continue to prevent dehydration. It is easier to stay on top of it than try to catch up.

- Fluids should be cooler than the air outside (55–72° Fahrenheit), but not ice cold or flavored, so they go down more easily.

- When exercising or in an event longer than an hour, your hydration should include carb and electrolyte replacement. If you are exercising less than an hour, you do not need to replace carbs and electrolytes. Water is fine.

- During intense exercise lasting longer than an hour, your body needs 30–60 grams of carbs per hour. This is equal to one of those glucose packs. More practically, this can be achieved by drinking 600–1200 ml per hour (1 ½ to 2 ½ bottles) of a 4–8 percent carb drink.

- The replacement fluid should contain 0.5–0.7 grams per liter of sodium to promote fluid retention and prevent excess loss of sodium from excess fluid intake.

MICRONUTRIENTS

Micronutrients are nutrients, including vitamins and minerals, that are needed in only small amounts. Regular exercise may increase our need for vitamins and minerals, which serve a variety of roles in energy production, the synthesis of hemoglobin (the part of blood that carries oxygen), bone health, immune function, muscle building after exercise, and protection from oxidative damage. (Oxidative damage occurs because our cells produce substances called "free radicals" when working or harmed, and these hurt the surrounding cells.) Just as with the macronutrients, insufficient intake of micronutrients affects your daily life and athletic performance.

Most of the time, we can get adequate amounts of vitamins and minerals from our diets if we are following the RDAs. The American Dietetic Association states that "no vitamin or mineral supplement should be required if an athlete is consuming adequate energy from a variety of foods to maintain body weight." Coupling exercise with a restrictive diet, with a diet that leaves out food groups, or with consumption of empty calories may result in insufficient vitamin and mineral intake. Age may also present a special challenge for absorbing enough vitamins and minerals because of low energy intake, impaired absorption, chronic medical problems, and medications.

Table 2 provides information of important vitamins and minerals for aging athletes.

WHEN TO EAT

The timing of meals can enhance athletic performance. For sustained calorie regulation and blood glucose (sugar) control, it is

Table 2. Important Vitamins and Minerals for the Aging Athlete

Vitamin/ Mineral	Function	Dietary Intake	Differences/Recommendations for Aging Athletes/Exercisers
Riboflavin	Energy metabolism	Women = 1.1 mg Men = 1.3 mg	Increased requirement for female endurance athletes. High carb diet may increase bacterial synthesis and decrease dietary need.
Vitamin B6	Amino acid and glycogen metabolism	Women = 1.5 mg Men = 1.7 mg	Age increases requirement. Inadequate B6 compromises immunity. Some authors suggest increased levels to 2.0 mg/day.
Vitamin B12	Nucleic acid metabolism; prevents anemia; required for RBC (red blood cell) synthesis	Women = 2.4 ug Men = 2.4 ug	Atrophic gastritis, common with aging, prevents B12 absorption and increases the risk of anemia. Vegetarians require 2.8 ug since B12 is found only in animal foods.
Folate	Amino acid metabolism; nucleic acid and RBC synthesis; prevents anemia	Women = 400 ug Men = 400 ug	Atrophic gastritis, common with aging, prevents folic acid absorption and increases the risk of anemia.
Vitamin D	Bone health; enhances calcium absorption; modulates immune function	Women 50–70 = 10 ug Women > 70 = 15 ug Men 50–70 = 10 ug Men > 70 = 15 ug	Older skin is less able to synthesis vitamin D, which is a steroid hormone that is produced less after menopause. Must supplement.
Vitamin E	Antioxidant: prevents oxidative damage	Women = 15 mg Men = 15 mg	Protects against cataracts, heart disease. Extra may not be necessary for athletes but some studies suggest increased intake to 100 mg for endurance sports.
Calcium	Bone health; blood clotting; muscle contraction; nerve conduction	Women = 1200 mg Men = 1200 mg	Protects against stress fractures. Atrophic gastritis decreases absorption. Lost via sweat.
Iron	RBC production; prevents anemia	Women = 8 mg Men = 8 mg	Iron stores increase with age so supplementation may be less necessary.

Adapted with permission from Campbell and Geik, "Nutritional considerations for the older athlete," *Nutrition* 20(7–8) (July-August 2004).

best to eat small meals throughout the day. If you are trying to use 500 calories more than you take in each day, it is best not to skip eating. Your body doesn't know you are trying to lose weight and simply recognizes the deprivation, thinks it is starving, and shifts into a storage mode.

A small pre-exercise, carbohydrate-rich snack within one hour of training has been shown to enhance performance. This little energy boost should be low in fat and fiber and have a moderate amount of protein. If you are a morning exerciser, try one bottle of sports drink prior to exercising since fasting through the night leaves your liver stores of fuel low. The first time you try this, make sure you are near a bathroom since some people tolerate food coupled with exercise better than others.

If you are into endurance exercise lasting three to four hours, your body will love carbs while you are exercising. Thirty to 60 grams of carbs per hour will extend your performance if you start taking them early in your race or workout. For long workouts, you should take carbs during the race because the liver runs out of stored sugar after about three hours. This fuel shortage is what makes people "hit the wall" in a marathon.

After a long workout, take your first carb boost in the first 30 minutes of recovery and then every two hours for four to six hours. This will result in a higher stored glycogen level than if you delayed eating for two hours.

NUTRITIONAL SUPPLEMENTS

Since the first recognition that nutrition matters in achieving peak performance, a multimillion dollar market has developed focusing on the athlete's and exerciser's desire to be the best. A

WANT TO LOSE BODY FAT? THEN EAT!

Starving will not make your body fat go away. Remember that thin does not mean fit. Skipping meals makes your body think it is starving and activates all your body's defenses that are meant to protect it from true starvation. Our bodies have developed a variety of strategies to store and hold on to calories more efficiently if they don't know when your next meal will be.

This response to meal skipping is called the "starvation response." It kicks in when women eat less than 800–1200 kilocalories and men eat less than 1200–1800 kilocalories per day. The starvation response results in a slowed metabolism. Your body uses its own muscle as fuel (remember that muscle takes more energy to metabolize normally without doing extra work), and calories are quickly converted to fat. If you slow your metabolism by going into starvation mode, you can still eat very little while exercising more because you are using very few calories to live.

A sure way to increase your metabolism is to increase your muscle to fat ratio, i.e., the C part of F.A.C.E., or carrying a load. Another way is to eat small meals every three hours. This approach works for several reasons:

- Food digestion itself burns a lot of calories.

- A steady stream of healthy mini-meals prevents desperate vending machine binges.

- Small meals control fat storage.

- Nutrients are effectively utilized.

- Complex carbohydrates plus lean proteins and "healthy" fats stabilize your blood glucose and insulin levels, preventing the post-lunch energy crashes.

- Muscles develop better and break down less with a steady flow of protein.

huge number of nutritional aids, herbal supplements, and diet pills claim to enhance performance or make you get fit quickly. This market is not well regulated; a supplement manufacturer may say anything it wants about its product as long as it does not claim to diagnose, cure, treat, or prevent disease. Many of the claims made on bottle labels or infomercials are unsupported by sound research. In other words, be careful what you put in your mouth. If you want to be the best you can be, you need to eat a balanced diet and hydrate well while minimizing severe weight loss.

Another hot topic today is the role of testosterone and growth hormone supplementation for age-related muscle decline. Both of these hormones are naturally occurring in the body and decline with age. Studies are ongoing as to the short- and long-term effects of taking these drugs. It appears that supplementation can increase low levels of both testosterone and growth hormone but will not increase levels above normal. Even this increase back to normal levels, however, seems to increase muscle mass but does not necessarily increase strength or overall function.

Two large studies in the United States and the Netherlands found similar declines of muscle strength and performance in men with high and low testosterone levels. In addition, studies show that the effects of supplemental testosterone on muscle strength and function are inconsistent and may not outweigh the possible risks of testosterone treatment, such as cardio-vascular disease, prostate cancer, and increased blood thickness. Most researchers currently conclude that much more research is necessary before widespread prescription of testosterone or growth hormone supplementation can be instituted.

THE VEGETARIAN EXERCISER

A vegetarian diet does not necessarily affect energy consumption. Vegetarians generally have a lower protein intake since plant protein is less easily digested than animal protein. Athletes should make sure they are getting 1.3–1.8 grams per kilogram of body weight of plant protein per day.

Vegetarian athletes can easily take in sufficient protein providing their diet is adequate in energy sources and contains a variety of plant-protein foods, such as legumes, grains, nuts, and seeds, according to D. Enette Larson-Meyer, PhD, a registered dietitian and member of the ADA's Dietetic Practice Group. For example, a male athlete weighing 80 kilograms and consuming 3600 calories would receive 1.41 grams per kilogram of body weight of protein from the average vegetarian diet and 1.2 grams per kilogram of body weight of protein from the average vegan diet. (A vegan diet contains no animal-derived protein sources. For example, vegans do not eat meat, fish, eggs, or dairy foods.) A 50-kilogram female athlete consuming 2200 calories per day would receive 1.38 grams per kilogram of body weight from a vegetarian diet and 1.21 grams per kilogram of body weight from a vegan diet. Therefore, most vegetarian athletes meet the requirements for endurance training without special meal planning. Strength-trained athletes (weight lifters, wrestlers, football players, or field throwers) or those with high training levels or low energy intakes may need to include more protein-rich foods. This is easily accomplished, Larson-Meyer says, by encouraging the athlete to add one to three servings of protein-rich foods to her current diet (e.g., a soy milk shake, lentils with spaghetti sauce, tofu added to a stir-fry, or garbanzo beans added to a salad).

If you are a vegetarian, be aware that vegetarians are at risk for low levels of certain vitamins and minerals, as discussed below.

B Vitamins

Vegetarian diets can provide the requirements for most B vitamins. Depending on the type of vegetarian diet, however, riboflavin and vitamin B12 are potential exceptions. Vitamin B12 has been studied for its effect on vegetarian athletic performance because of its function in maintaining the blood and nervous systems. In fact, injections of B12 are still used by some athletes and coaches because of the belief that it increases oxygen delivery, which in turn will enhance endurance. Since cobalamin—the active form of B12—is found exclusively in animal products, vegan athletes need to regularly consume B12-fortified foods, which include nutritional yeast and those brands of soymilk, breakfast cereals, and meat analogs that are fortified with B12. Vegetarians who consume eggs, cheese, milk, or yogurt receive an ample supply of this vitamin.

Several studies have suggested that riboflavin needs may be increased in people with borderline riboflavin status who are beginning an exercise program. Since riboflavin intakes are reportedly low in some vegans, active vegetarians who avoid dairy products should learn the plant sources of riboflavin to ensure adequate intake. Plant sources of riboflavin include whole grain cereals, soybeans, dark green leafy vegetables, avocados, nuts, and sea vegetables.

Antioxidant Vitamins

Vitamins C and E and carotene are called antioxidant vitamins because they may protect against exercise-induced "oxidative stress." Several scientific reviews detail the benefits of antioxidant supplements in protecting our bodies against the harmful effects of free radical damage. However, studies have not shown that these vitamins enhance exercise performance. Vegetarian athletes may have an advantage over non-vegetarians since antioxidants are readily obtained from a diet rich in vegetables, nuts, seeds, and vegetable oils, which vegetarians consume.

Vitamin D

Vitamin D is essential for the absorption of calcium and phosphorus and for bone formation. Lack of adequate vitamin D may manifest itself in unexplained muscle pain or weakness or low calcium balance. Vitamin D is present in oily fish, eggs, and dairy products in variable amounts. It is not found in plant foods. However, vegans can obtain vitamin D from vegetable margarines, some soy milks, and certain other foods that are fortified with the vitamin. Vitamin D is also synthesized by the skin when it is exposed to sunlight. Synthesis of vitamin D in this way is usually adequate to supply all the body's requirements. Most vegans will obtain sufficient vitamin D providing they spend time outdoors on bright days. Fortified foods further ensure adequate amounts. Vegans who may be confined indoors may need to take vitamin D supplements.

Iron

All athletes, particularly female endurance athletes, are at risk of iron depletion and iron deficiency anemia. Iron loss is increased in some athletes, particularly heavily training endurance athletes, because they are especially prone to gastrointestinal bleeding, heavy sweating, and hemolysis (the destruction of red blood cells), all of which cause iron loss.

Insufficient iron intake or reduced absorption, however, are the most probable causes of poor iron status. Some studies have found that female vegetarian runners had a similar iron intake but lower iron status than nonvegetarian runners. Most of the iron in a vegetarian diet is not as absorbable as that in meat. This may be of significance since low iron stores even without anemia have been associated with decreased endurance.

In most cases, vegetarian athletes can achieve proper iron status without iron supplementation, according to the Vegetarian

Nutrition Dietetic Practice Group of the ADA. However, vegetarians need to be educated about plant sources of iron and factors that enhance and interfere with iron absorption. For example, an athlete who consumes beans at lunch while drinking milk or tea could be advised to replace this beverage with citrus fruit juice to enhance iron absorption at that meal. In some cases, vegetarian athletes may temporarily require supplements to build up or maintain iron stores. Athletes taking iron supplements should have their iron status monitored because of the potential association between iron status and chronic disease.

Calcium

Low calcium intake has been associated with an increased risk of stress fractures and low bone density, particularly in female athletes who are not menstruating. The major source of calcium in Western diets is generally milk and dairy products. Vegans can obtain adequate calcium from plant foods. Good sources include tofu, leafy green vegetables, watercress, dried fruits, seeds, and nuts. Also, white bread is fortified with calcium, as are some soy milks. Hard water can also provide significant amounts of calcium.

Recommendations for active vegetarian men and premenopausal women are not different from the general RDA for adults, which is 800 mg. Calcium intake, however, is one of many factors associated with calcium balance and accounts for only 11 percent of its variation. Urinary calcium excretion, on the other hand, accounts for 51 percent of the variation in calcium balance and is influenced by dietary protein, sodium, and possibly phosphoric acid intakes. There is evidence to suggest that vegans (and possibly vegetarians who consume little dairy) may have lower calcium requirements because of their lower intakes of animal protein, total protein, and sodium, which increase kidney calcium excretion. However, until more is known about calcium requirements in this group, it is prudent that all athletes meet the RDA for calcium.

Zinc

Although little is known regarding the zinc status of vegetarian athletes, there may be cause for concern since the absorption of zinc from plant foods is somewhat lower than from animal products. Vegetarian sources of zinc include legumes, hard cheeses, whole grain products, wheat germ, fortified cereals, nuts, tofu, and miso.

STRATEGIC EATING

Strategically eating begins like strategically exercising—by making small changes daily. You need to think about what you eat and slowly begin to change your diet as necessary. Now that we have talked about your exercise output connection, the important role your mind plays in facing your future, and your nutritional input, the next chapter talks about the mind-body connection and the important role your mind plays in facing your future.

HOME**WORK**

This chapter was packed full of information. Simply start by being aware of what you are putting into your body. Keep a log in your PDA or Day-Timer and at the end of a week, look it over. When are you skipping meals? When are you overdoing it? What are you doing right?

KEEP AN EYE ON PORTION SIZE

What is the difference between portions and servings? A "portion" can be thought of as the amount of a specific food you choose to eat for dinner, a snack, or another eating occasion. Portions, of course, can be bigger or smaller than the recommended food servings.

A "serving" is a unit of measure used to describe the amount of food recommended from each food group. It is the amount of food listed on the Nutrition Facts panel on packaged food or the amount of food recommended in the Food Guide Pyramid and the Dietary Guidelines for Americans, released by the U.S. government.

For example, six to 11 servings of whole grains are recommended daily. A recommended serving of whole grains would be one slice of bread of a half cup of rice or pasta. (Download the Serving Size Card at the website *hp2010.nhlbihin.net/portion/servingcard7.pdf* for more examples of recommended serving sizes.) People often confuse the recommendation to mean six to 11 portions with no regard to size. It is *not* six to 11 portions where a portion could mean a large bowl of pasta rather than a half cup. Keep an eye on portion size to see how your portions compare with the recommended amounts.

Check out the Menu Planner at the website *hp2010.nhlbihin.net/ menuplanner/menu.cgi* to see examples of appropriate portions and serving sizes. The Menu Planner can help you create your own meals or add up your daily calorie intake. You can also check the sample menus for weight loss at the website *www.nhlbi.nih.gov/health/public/heart/obesity/lose_wt/sampmenu.htm* . The sample menus can also help you create reduced calorie meal plans. These items use the servings recommended by the American Dietetic Association (ADA) Food Exchange List. The servings recommended by the ADA exchange list may differ from the Nutrition Facts panel and the Dietary Guidelines for Americans. See the ADA Food Exchange List at *www.nhlbi .nih.gov/health/public/heart/obesity/lose_wt/fd_exch.htm* to give yourself more choices.

"Physical fitness is not only one of the most important keys to a healthy body; it is the basis of dynamic and creative intellectual activity. The relationship between the soundness of the body and the activities of the mind is subtle and complex. Much is not yet understood. But we do know what the Greeks knew: that intelligence and skill can only function at the peak of their capacity when the body is healthy and strong; that hardy spirits and tough minds usually inhabit sound bodies."

—John F. Kennedy,
   in *Sports Illustrated* (December 1960)

CHAPTER **ELEVEN**

"In the Mouth of the Wolf"

Creating Your Mental Edge

"In bocca al lupo . . . in bocca al lupo . . . crepe lupo!" *In bocca al lupo* means "in the mouth of the wolf." This is the mantra I repeat over and over at the end of a long or faster-than-usual race to keep myself going. It is the mental edge of my game. We all need a mantra, that mental edge, to keep us going when our bodies have taken up camp with the enemy. The mental edge is important because at some point, it is all in your head—whether you are simply trying to motivate yourself to step away from the couch each day or run to the next lightpole before you stop to walk, or when you are at the end of a long, hard race and need to "twist the towel," if you will, to get the last drops of energy out of your body.

So here I am at mile 20 of my last marathon—6.2 miles to go, and I began feeling tired at mile 18. By mile 20, my legs are still my allies, but my core and buttocks are screaming since I am a typical runner and don't spend enough time working on them. The streets are filled with well-meaning fans waving, cheering, and yelling "you are almost there"—but 6.2 miles is *not* almost there. As stated previously, *in bocca al lupo* means "in the mouth of the wolf." I feel like I am in the mouth of the wolf, facing down this physical and mental challenge I am 20 miles into. I hear the muffled sound of the crowd around me, but I am all in my head and I hear myself talking. This race is bigger than this moment. I've been training daily for six months, and yet it is all about this moment. "In bocca al lupo," I repeat," and my triumphant response is "crepe lupo": *slay the wolf*. I will not be overtaken in this moment, and I keep running.

Believe it or not, I borrowed "In bocca al lupo . . . crepe lupo" from several of my opera singer friends. It is their version of "break a leg." Imagine you are one voice about to take the stage where you will battle, without microphones, to not only be heard but brilliantly heard as you vie to resonate over the voices of an 80-piece orchestra, 30 chorus members, and several other principal singers before more than 2,000 people in the hall. The opera singer stands in the wings of the stage, viewing her playing field. If she fails, it is a public failure, known in the hall, the newspapers, and around the world. She is looking into the mouth of the wolf. "In bocca al lupo," one singer says to another. "Crepe lupo" is the firm reply as defeat is not an option.

Choosing a mantra, a word, a phrase, a name, or a song that means "I will not be defeated in this moment" is one important part of mental training.

My patients have the benefit of developing their mental toughness with the help of our mental training consultant, Dr. Aimee Kimball, director of mental training at the UPMC Center for Sports Medicine. She routinely assists our athletes of all ages and activity levels to raise the bar of their on-the-field and off-the-field performance. I have taken notes on her advice and she has encouraged me to share them with you in this chapter.

WHAT IS MENTAL TRAINING?

Mental training, also known as sport psychology or performance enhancement, is similar to physical skills training in that the goal is to prepare athletes to consistently perform their best. While physical training focuses on teaching the body proper execution of skills, mental training focuses on teaching the mind to remove mental barriers that might hinder your performance. Mental training is an individualized program that teaches you how to identify and recreate your ideal mindset in order to perform your best in competition and in practice. Mental training gives athletes the knowledge and ability to control their thinking, their emotions, and, in turn, their performance. Teams can benefit from mental training as well. Mental training gives the individual athlete and teams the competitive edge they need to take their game to a higher level.

DISPELLING SOME MENTAL TRAINING MYTHS

Many athletes and coaches claim that at least 60 percent of their sport is mental; however, most people spend little if any time working on the mental aspects of their sport. Coaches say one reason for this is that there is not enough time for physical training, let alone mental training. While the schedules of coaches and athletes are limited, after the initial learning stage, mental training does not require a lot of extra time. In fact, mental training is most effective when it can be incorporated into everyday practice and competition, enhancing the quality of both.

Another reason coaches and athletes give for not working on the mental game is that mental training is only for elite athletes. While it is true that many of the top athletes in the world do engage in mental training, athletes of all ages and levels can benefit from enhancing their ability to control their mind. Whether they are building confidence, increasing concentration, or controlling their anxiety, athletes of all ages and abilities can use a variety of mental training techniques both in sport and in life.

Another common myth is that mental training is only for athletes with problems. On the contrary, mental training is most effective when it is used to *prevent* performance problems from occurring rather than to provide a quick fix to a performance slump.

HOW DO YOU RAISE THE BAR?

As you are thinking about your own mental edge, work through the following mental training skills.

Consistently Perform at Your Peak

- Ask yourself what you can do to make today better than yesterday. Work on this.
- Don't settle for being comfortable. Striving for more enhances performance.
- Don't settle for what's "good enough for today." Go above and beyond the minimum expected of you.

Know What Drives You and Stay Focused on These Motivators

- How do you define excellence?
- What are you trying to accomplish?
- What drives you to be better?
- What do you like about what you are doing?
- What is your view of yourself?

Set Goals for Success

- Don't just set out to "try your hardest." Set specific goals so you can measure whether or not you accomplished them.
- Make sure your goals are challenging but realistic and know when you want to accomplish them.
- Focus small, don't get ahead of yourself, and take it one thing at a time.

- Focus on process goals (the fundamentals you need to perform well), not only on outcome goals.
- Set goals for every aspect of your life.
- Keep goals positive.
- Set up a support system, tell people your goals, and ask them to reinforce your efforts.
- Write your goals down. This is very important!

Know the Types of Goals

- Realize that on a day-to-day basis, you will see the most improvement by focusing on the fundamentals that are necessary to succeed, not on the final result you want to achieve. Thus, setting goals is extremely important in helping you to reach your peak. There are three sets of goals you need to know about:

  1. *Outcome goals* focus on the results (winning, being the best). This type of goal is motivating but usually outside your immediate control.

  2. *Performance goals* focus on improvements relative to your own past performance (e.g., time improvement).

  3. *Process goals* are related to procedures engaged in during performance (workout plan, stride, focus). You totally control process goals and the focus is on self-improvement, so they keep you motivated in the face of obstacles.

Use Your Goals to Motivate You

- Focus on and reward your process goals.
- Develop goal buddies.

- Establish daily reminders (for instance, you can use a motto).
- Establish goal-focused workouts (workout plans that move toward your overall goal).
- Picture your desired achievements.
- Have a weekly theme.

Develop the Midas Touch

- Don't sell yourself short. Make today your day.
- Ask yourself: "What can I improve upon today?"
- Focus on what you want to accomplish in every situation.
- Know what you are working toward.

MORE THAN JUST PERFORMANCE

While mental training is most commonly used to help individual or team performance, several other issues can be addressed through mental training. First, mental training can assist athletes who are injured in dealing with stress, in expediting the rehabilitation process, and in mentally preparing to return to competition. Second, a mental training consultant can help to educate parents and coaches on ways to enhance a young athlete's sport experience. Talking with groups about their influence on athletes' lives not only helps to ensure a positive sport experience for the athletes but also assists in opening the lines of communication among parents, coaches, and athletes. Third, mental training can assist athletes outside of sport in developing life skills, working through major life decisions, and transitioning out of sport. Dr. Kimball can be reached to help you maximize your performance through her website *sportsmedicine.upmc.com/MentalTrainingProgram.htm* or via email at *kimballac@upmc.edu.*

As you proceed toward the last few chapters of this book, equipped to take control and age in the best possible way through exercise, look into the mouth of your wolf and F.A.C.E. your future without fear. Crepe lupo.

HOME**WORK**

Set a goal. Fill out the following lines.

*   My long-term goal is: _____

    _____

*   My goal for this week is: _____

    _____

*   What can I do to achieve this? _____

    _____

*   What obstacles might I face, and how can I overcome them? _____

    _____

*   What will result from my achieving this goal? _____

    _____

Make a statement.

- My mission this year is to: _____

  _____

- Every day I will: _____

  _____

"Even if you are on the right track,
you'll get run over if you just sit there."

—Will Rogers

CHAPTER TWELVE

When the Shoe Fits, Wear It

At this point, you have so much inspiration you are probably raring to go, and if you are, then just go right now before the surge of energy passes. I hope you have been flexing, walking, resisting, and balancing as you prepared yourself through this book. One additional bit of preparation not to be overlooked is your equipment. I don't want you to add "I have nothing to wear" to the list of excuses that can crop up for not working out, so let's talk about the gear you need—shoes and tops.

SHOES

I have run many races with my 69-year-old father, who told you his story in Chapter 1. I am always fascinated and amused to watch how deliberately he addresses his equipment before a race. Since he is a longtime masters athlete, I decided to get his take on how he chooses footwear and how to organize yourself for fitness after 40 and for a road race. He responded in the form of a letter to you:

> Hello, fitness after 40 enthusiasts:
>
> Welcome to a great life. Now that you have made the decision to take control of the quality of your life and the aging process, I would like to give you a few thoughts and hints about the equipment you need.
>
> Beginning to exercise on a consistent basis requires very little equipment. Most of the equipment is inexpensive and readily available. You probably have most of it in your dresser already. The hard and fast rule concerning equipment is that it must be comfortable. If any part of your equipment is uncomfortable when you put it on, it will get really uncomfortable when you are exercising in it.
>
> What do you need? The first piece of equipment you need and the most important piece of equipment you must have is a pair of shoes. The decision you make concerning which shoes, what brand, and what type of shoes to buy should take some time and effort. There are so many brands and styles of shoes that finding the brand and style that is best for you may be difficult. When you buy your shoes, I suggest that you go to a company and salesperson that is familiar with and knowledgeable about running shoes and walking shoes. This person will be able to fit you properly.

Buy a pair of shoes that is specific for your sport. There are walking shoes, running shoes, tennis shoes, and good old sneakers for tooling around the house. Know what you need. If you are walking, you can get away with a pair of running shoes, but a pair of walking shoes is usually too stiff for running. If you are buying a pair of running shoes, go to a shop that specializes in running shoes and has staff that actually run. They will analyze the shoe's fit on your foot and talk to you about what kind of workout you do. If you don't know where to find a running shoe store, go to *www.runnersworld.com* and hit the bar for "shoes and gear." Under "store finder," you will find stores listed by state.

There are a few things that you should remember when you are at the store buying your shoes. Your shoes should caress your feet. You should also look for cushioning and support. Buy athletic shoes that run one to two sizes larger than your street shoes. You need more room in the toe area and mid-foot area. These shoes are just built that way. You also need more room because during exercise, your feet will get bigger and need room to expand. You also do not want to inhibit the circulation in your feet. In addition, you probably do not want the most expensive shoe you can get, and you certainly do not want the cheapest shoe on the market. A mid-priced shoe is usually the best. You can usually get a pair for $80 to $100.

Take your time in the shoe store because this piece of equipment can make or break your workout. If you have a pair of shoes that you walk or run around in already, it is best to bring them with you so the staff can look at the tread and how you wear out your shoes. If you wear inserts, bring them too since the staff can use all this information to help you choose the best shoe for your foot. Also, make sure you take the socks you are going to wear while exercising. You want to guarantee a perfect fit.

Very quickly, there will be several pairs of shoes around you on the floor, and probably two or three pairs that you have decided you might want. Try the first pair on. How do they feel? Walk around in them. If the store has a treadmill, walk a few minutes on it while wearing the shoes. If you feel any rough spot, tight area, or discomfort, take them off and try the next pair. If the shoes are too tight, you will end up pounding your big toenails and losing them, rubbing your skin raw, compressing the nerves that wrap around your sole, or having numb toes. Keep trying different pairs on until your feet are caressed and you are completely happy with the shoes.

In short, be very particular when you are buying your shoes. They are the foundation of all that you do. If your feet are not comfortable, all other parts of your body will be affected. The wrong shoes may cause discomfort and injuries. If you have purchased a pair of shoes that you like, stick with them.

My best advice is to be deliberate, take your time, and don't skimp on the price of the shoes.

See you on the road,
Gene Wright

I want to emphasize a few things my dad mentioned. First, our feet do change considerably as we age, and for women, as we have children. They get both longer and wider. Let the shoe clerk measure both of your feet while you are standing. You may be surprised at your new size. Also, many exercise shoes come in multiple widths per length. Aging causes the most problems with the front (forefoot) of the foot, including pain (metatarsalgia) and bunions. This makes the width and height of the front of the shoe key. Even if the clerk measures your foot and brings out that size, if it doesn't fit correctly, experiment until you find one that does. Shoe sizing varies per company. If your feet measured different sizes, begin trying on the bigger size.

Athletic shoes are designed with the different foot types in mind. In general, there are three foot types: the normal, the flat (pronated), and the high arch (supinated). Each has different issues. To determine which type you are, take the "wet test." With a damp foot, step onto a piece of colored paper or cardboard. If your footprint looks like a regular foot, you probably have normal feet. If the footprint looks almost rectangular, you have a flat foot. If you see only the ball, toes, and heel with little in between, you have a high arched foot.

If you have a normal foot, you will have minimal calluses and can wear any shoe that has moderate support. The flat foot rolls in excessively. This can cause calluses, bunions, neuromas (masses surrounding nerves between your toes), plantar fasciitis, and stress fractures of the bones in the forefoot. Flat feet require maximum support with motion-control shoes and firm mid-soles. This means that the shoes will have strong plastic heel counters, firm plastic inserts in the mid-foot portion, and a wider stable base of support. They do not need highly cushioned shoes. Flat-footed exercisers should look for labels that say "motion-control." Motion control means that the shoe actually is stiffer and does part of the job your foot should do to stay stable.

On the other hand, a high arched foot has poor shock absorption. This leads to more ankle sprains, pain under the big toe (sesamoiditis), calluses, and hammertoes (where the second through fifth toes bend up and hit the top of the shoe). High arched feet need shoes that allow plenty of motion and cushioning. People with high arched feet should look for labels that say "absorb," "gel," "air," and "hydroflow." The best way to get the right footwear is to shop at a specialty shoe store instead of a department store.

SUPPORT ON TOP

For women, the sports bra is key after shoes. There are many different types today, and just like you do with everyday bras, you should try them on and consider several features. A sports bra must not simply smash your breasts against your body. It must support your figure. While in the store, jump up and down, jog in place, raise and lower your arms. How does it feel? Are you still inside it? Is it comfortable? Does it dig into your skin or bind you up? Finally, fabric is important. Cotton generally stays wet and cold, so I would look toward the new synthetic blends. There are many high-tech fabrics that are capable of wicking moisture away from your body so that it will evaporate.

For both men and women, shorts, tops, and jackets are the basic elements that follow next. For your first foray off the couch, you can throw on whatever cotton T-shirt you have around. As you get serious, however, you want to choose comfortable, skimming workout clothes that are not baggy. Clothes that are loose fitting or too short or tight will make using gym machines or getting on the floor difficult. Don't overdress. If you stay cool, you are more likely to continue exercising. Again, when you are buying these clothes, make sure there are no areas that are rubbing or chafing your skin.

Let me tell you, raw skin and sweat hurts. One extra not to forget is body lubricant. Silicone-based ointment works nicely to prevent chafing under the arms, between the thighs, or anywhere that rubs.

Workout clothes are primarily functional, but a spiffy workout outfit can be part of your strategic plan, and putting it on can be a signal to your mind that you are ready to work out.

HOME**WORK**

If you are just stepping off the couch for the first time in years, go find your athletic shoes. After you dig them off the floor of the back of your closet, put them on and walk right into an athletic shoe store to make your first financial investment in F.A.C.E.-ing your future. Let these spanking new shoes be an inspiration to you.

If you have a functional pair of shoes, look ahead to the end of the first six weeks of your daily investment in fitness after 40 and mark a day on your calendar when you are going to reward your consistent progress by getting a new pair of shoes. We really do need this kind of goal and reward system to keep us going and looking forward.

If you are already a consistent exerciser, think back to when you bought your current shoes. If you are a runner and you have run more than 500 miles on them, then run to the store now. If you can't figure out how many miles they have lasted, then use six months as a time guide. For the average 20-mile-a-week runner, it takes six months to run 500 miles.

"If fitness came in a bottle,
everyone would have a great body."

—Cher

CHAPTER THIRTEEN

How to Choose a Gym and Personal Trainer

You do not need a gym to work out. Any space and your own weight will do. Sometimes, however, it is easier to stay motivated if you have a place to go and a variety of activities to do. I encourage my patients to join a gym for just this reason. For some, affording the membership is an issue. My answer to this excuse for not exercising is to have the cable turned off and invest the money in a gym membership.

CHOOSING A GYM

In order to make the most of your money, here are a few tips on choosing the best place.

• *Location, location, location*. It doesn't matter if you are thinking about joining the Taj Mahal of gyms; if it is not easily accessible to you, you will not go frequently. You think you will now, when you are romanced by the gym's bells and whistles, but you won't. Choose a gym that is less than 10 minutes from your home or work and one that has easy access to parking.

• *What is your bottom line?* Think about how you like to exercise. Are you a class joiner, a spinner, a runner, a lap swimmer? Do you like pilates, yoga, aerobics? Your gym should have a wide variety of activities that you like to do. It must also have floor space for stretching with an abundance of exercise toys such as exercise balls, stools, and rubber tubing. It should have both machine and free weights.

• *Is it equipped?* Does the gym have adequate numbers of solo cardio machines and weight equipment to ensure that you won't wait forever? Does the equipment accommodate all skill levels and sizes? Is the aerobics floor wooden or suspended? (Both are easier on the joints than concrete.) What condition is the equipment in? Is it clean? Run your finger along the equipment. If it is dirty or sticky, beware. Are there bottles of disinfectant near the equipment groups? You want a gym that expects members to towel off the equipment with disinfectant after they use it. Alternatively, there should be an attendant who does this after every client. Look down at the carpet and the showers. Are they clean?

• *Try it on for size*. Most gyms give potential members weekly passes to try the place out. Visit during a time you are likely to work out. When you visit, look around at whom you will be exercising with. Do you feel comfortable? Is staff available to answer your questions or assist you? If the idea of working out among professional hard bodies makes you feel shy, you might try your local YMCA, community center, or college athletic center instead. For women who are uncomfortable working out around men, choose a gym that allows only women or has designated women-only areas. Does the gym offer fitness testing and program orientation?

- *Open all night.* While most gyms are not open 24/7, they must be open early and stay open late to accommodate you. This includes the weekends.

- *Cash out of pocket.* Gyms usually charge an initiation fee and a monthly fee. Does the monthly fee include everything, or will you pay extra for the "good stuff" or to be there during prime time? Can you bring a guest, and if so, how often and for what fee?

- *The staff.* Besides having a good attitude, the staff at a gym should be trained in both first aid and CPR. They should also be certified by an organization such as the American Council on Exercise, the American College of Sports Medicine, or the YMCA/YWCA.

CONSIDERING YOUR PERSONAL FITNESS TRAINER

Sometimes we all need a helping hand, and a personal fitness trainer can be just the right addition to your fitness plan. A personal trainer can assist you in evaluating your fitness level, planning a program, and keeping you motivated. Sometimes you need someone standing over your shoulder to push yourself to the next level. In addition, a personal trainer should be able to educate you about F.A.C.E.-ing your future.

You must be careful, however, to choose a trainer who understands what *you* want to accomplish and the unique qualities of the mature athlete and active ager. The trainer must understand that you are not merely a bad sequel to your 20-year-old self but are in fact unique. I recommend finding a trainer who has previously worked with masters athletes and adult onset exercisers. Interview the trainer to find out if she believes that fitness after 40 is possible. Although there are many great therapists and trainers out there, you would be surprised by how many of them buy into the notion that we should all just slow down when we reach a certain arbitrary age. Such a belief affects how they will work with you.

Just like any service, one great way to find a personal trainer is to ask your friends, family, business associates, etc., if they are working with anyone they like. You can also watch the personal trainers who work at your gym and observe how they work with people. If you see someone you like, ask to talk to him about your goals. You also want to choose a personal trainer who is certified. You can find a list of certified personal trainers online at *www.acsm.org, www.ideafit.com*, or *www.nsca-lift.org*.

If you decide to hire a personal trainer, do so for a short period of time first. Then, if you are achieving your goals with him, you can purchase additional sessions. It would be unfortunate to buy a six-month package of training sessions only to find out you don't get along with your trainer or he doesn't understand your goals.

The International Council on Active Aging (ICAA) has put together a great guide for choosing a personal fitness trainer qualified to work with you. It is found at their website, *www.icaa.cc*.

It consists of specific questions you can use to interview your potential trainer and the responses you are looking for.

Here is a list of general areas to consider:

- *Education.* Your trainer must be certified by the American College of Sports Medicine, American Council on Exercise, or the National Strength and Conditioning Association. Ideally, she would also have a degree in exercise science or a related college degree.

- *Experience.* Although everyone has to start somewhere, try to choose a trainer who has several years of experience in relationship to your specific goals. If you are a cyclist, you want someone who understands your sport; if you have specific medical conditions, you want a trainer who has had experience with other people with these conditions. Does the trainer have experience helping people in your age group maximize their performance? Does the trainer understand the strategies for injury prevention in the masters athlete?

- *Personality and professionalism.* You will be working closely with your personal trainer, so does he seem like a person whose personality meshes with yours? Does he listen to you and what your goals are, or do you sense that he has his own agenda? Does he keep up with the latest technology? What does he expect of you?

- *Logistics.* Does this trainer come to your particular gym, and will she come to your home or local park? What hours is she available? How does she prefer to be paid? Does she have liability insurance?

- *Take a trial run.* Before committing to a package of training sessions, take a trial run. Evaluate how you feel working with this person. Does he listen to you? Are the workouts varied and in line with what you have read in this book? Did he give you hints about form and lifestyle as you worked out?

HOME**WORK**

If you decide to hire a personal trainer, do not be afraid to ask the questions outlined above. Remember that you are entrusting your body to this person and you want to make sure you are the focus of his interest. You can help your trainer to help you by putting some thought into what kind of fitness goals you want to achieve. As discussed Chapter 11, setting and writing down goals makes it easier to achieve them.

Be able to tell your trainer the answers to the following questions:

- *Specifically, what do you want to achieve by hiring him?* For instance, you could say: "I want to lose five pounds in the next five weeks," "I want to be supervised while I work through the four components of F.A.C.E.-ing my future," "I want to work up to walking three miles," or "I want to evaluate my muscle weaknesses and focus on strengthening them."

- *Exactly what do you want your body to look like?* If you see a picture of the kind of legs, abdomen, or arms you would like to have, bring the picture to show him.

- *How much time will you commit to achieving these goals?* For instance: "I can meet with you for one hour four times a week, and one session must be on a Saturday."

- *How do you like to learn?* Do you like a lot of demonstration or coaching? Think also about how you are motivated. Do you respond to coaching that is more encouraging (for instance, "Great job, that was fantastic form. In the next set, let's turn it up a notch"). Or do you prefer coaching that is more critical in style (for instance, "Your form was off, focus on the next set"). This is important. If criticism does not motivate you, you will resent your trainer using this method and you will not progress as well as if he used a more encouraging style. The reverse is also true.

"It's a dream until you write it down,
and then it's a goal."

—Anonymous

14

Onward! Putting a Plan Together

In the last 13 chapters, you have gained the knowledge and tools you need to F.A.C.E. your future of active aging and maximize your performance as you go. This final chapter is meant to help you put all the information together in a plan. I am going to offer you a suggestion for getting started, but I hope that you will use it only as a template and think through what you have learned to design a schedule that will work for *you*. It is easy to tear a workout out of the pages of one of the many health magazines and promise to follow it, but the reality is that such a workout usually goes nowhere. By investing your time in strategic planning, you *own* your regimen. And if you take ownership, you are more likely to follow through.

MAKING A PLAN

Making a plan will help you get started. And as Mark Twain said, "The secret of getting ahead is getting started. The secret of getting started is breaking your complex overwhelming tasks into small manageable tasks, and then starting on the first one."

Here are the basic steps you need to follow to make your plan.

- *What do you want to do in the next 12 weeks?* Set a distance, choose a race, or otherwise decide what you want to do. Think about your future.

- *See your doctor and get permission to start exercising.* Answer the health assessment questions in Chapter 5.

- *Make exercising nonnegotiable.* Plan around your exercise time; don't just fit it in if you can—you won't.

- *Set up a way to be accountable.* Tell all your family, coworkers, even strangers what you are going to do. Write it in your calendar, set an alarm in your PDA, put it up as your screensaver.

- *Establish a reward.* Feeling great is going to be an amazing reward, but perhaps you should buy yourself a special treat. Better yet, plan to race in some vacation spot.

- *Make a plan and write it down.* Do this today. Why wait? See the plan guide in Table 3. Remember to include:
- F—flexibility: daily
- A—aerobic: three to five times, moderately, per week
- C—carrying a load: three times per week (working the same muscle group only every other day)
- E—equilibrium: daily

**Table 3. An Example of an Easy Six-Week Plan for
Getting off the Couch and onto Your Future**

	Monday	Tuesday	Wednesday	Thursday	Friday	Saturday	Sunday	Goal
Week 0						A	A	Start with aerobic 3×/week
Week 1		A		FA		FA	F	Add flexibility daily
Week 2	FC or F	FA or FAC	FC or F	FA or FAC	FC or F	FA or FAC	F	Add resistance (carrying a load) 3×/week
Week 3	FCE or FE	FAE or FACE	FCE or FE	FAE or FACE	FCE or FE	FAE or FACE	FE	Add equilibrium daily
Week 4	FCE or FE	FAE or FACE	FCE or FE	FAE or FACE	FCE or FE	FAE or FACE	FE	Increase A by 10 percent or add an A day
Week 5	FCE or FE	FAE or FACE	FCE or FE	FAE or FACE	FCE or FE	FAE or FACE	FE	Increase A by 10 percent
Week 6	FCE or FE	FAE or FACE	FCE or FE	FAE or FACE	FCE or FE	FAE or FACE	FE	Increase A by 10 percent or add an A day

F = flexibility (Chapter 4), A = aerobic (Chapter 5), C = carry a load (Chapter 6), E = equilibrium (Chapter 7)

Here is an explanation of what to do in each week of the sample plan shown in Table 3.

* *Week 0.* Make your plan, starting on a weekend when you have more time. Test your shoes. Always warm up for five to 10 minutes prior to exercise. Do 15 to 30 minutes of brisk aerobic exercise by walking, cycling, stair climbing, elliptical—anything that gets your heart rate up.

- *Week 1*. This week, you are going to continue your new aerobic habit on three days. In the example in the table, A (aerobic work) is done on Tuesday, Thursday, and Saturday, but you can choose any three days you wish. If you need to do A two days in a row to get it in, I would rather you do so than skip a workout. Better, however, would be to do a lower extremity aerobic workout one day followed by an upper body aerobic workout the next day (e.g., running on day 1 and swimming on day 2). On the second aerobic day of the week, you are going to add F—flexibility *after* you exercise. Stretch only warm muscles.

Note: In my example weeks, you will notice that a Tuesday-Thursday-Saturday or a Monday-Wednesday-Friday schedule is used for A and C. The F and E components are daily.

- *Week 2*. This week, you are going to C—carry a load, or resistance training. Three days is enough. You can either do this on alternate days when you are not doing the aerobic work (Monday, Wednesday, and Friday), or you can do it on the same day as your aerobic workout. I find that it is easier to do the aerobic work first and then the resistance work, with the flexibility work at the end all on the same day. This week, you are doing the flexibility work every day. For instance, in Week 2, on Monday if you do FC, then Tuesday, you would do FA. If on Monday you do only F, then Tuesday you would do FAC.

- *Week 3*. You are now F.A.C.E.-ing your future by adding the E—equilibrium exercises throughout the day or as part of your concentrated workout. The equilibrium exercises, like the flexibility exercises, are best done every day. Continue the A—aerobic and C—carrying components of your workout. If you are not able to fit it all in according to the way you planned your schedule, do your best. Doing something is better than nothing. Remember: Accentuate the positive. No defeatist self-talk. In Week 3, if you do FCE on Monday, then Tuesday is FAE. If you do only FE on Monday, then Tuesday is packed with F.A.C.E.

- *Weeks 4–6*. During Weeks 4–6, continue your F.A.C.E. regimen. It seems like a lot, but if you move steadily through your workout without a lot of standing around in between the different parts, you can fit it all in about an hour—for instance, 30 minutes aerobic with the first five minutes as warm-up, 15 minutes of resistance work with the equilibrium exercises done during your rest periods between lifting sets, 15 minutes of stretching, which also acts as your cool down. Each week, either increase your A—aerobic time by at least 10 percent or add a day (three to five days is the goal).

Remember, as we spoke about in Chapter 5, make a specific strategic plan for each day of the week that includes date, time, location, activity, intensity, and duration/distance. For instance, using the sample plan in Table 3, the plan for Tuesday of Week 2 might be:

Tuesday (FA) 5:30 p.m.: North Park Circle—10-minute warm-up with brisk walk, 30-minute jog with heart rate around 70 percent of maximum, 15-minute stretch of lower extremities. Note to self: Take gym bag to job and work out on the way home.

If you are a detail person and like to check off a list of what you have done, you could make a chart like the one on the next two pages to track the specific exercises you did every day. You can download this chart at www.fitnessafter40book.com.

It may be rocky at first as the movements, equipment, and training in general are unfamiliar, and you may consider hanging it all up. Don't do it. Feeling awkward is very normal, but soon you will develop a routine or a rhythm to your workouts and you will flow from one component to the next. I like to do my aerobic and resistance work all on the same day. I warm up, run or spin on a cycle, get a quick drink, and then go immediately to lifting with my arms and legs. I then stretch . . . and it feels so good.

Date	M	Tue	W	Th	F	Sat	Sun	Notes
F—flex: Hold 30 sec x 4 rep **daily**								
Neck								
Shoulder								
Roll								
Trapezius								
Chest								
Shoulder								
Triceps								
Lower								
Back								
Hip Flex								
Hamstring								
Quadricep								
Calves								
A—aerobic: 30 min × **3 days/wk**								
Dynamic Warm-Up								
Hip circles								
Lunge								
Inchworm								
Heel/toe walks								
Skip								
Rhythm bounding								
Other								
30-Minute Aerobic Workout								
Time/Distance								
C—carry a load 3 days/wk: muscle groups OR FITNESS to GO								
Lower back—list # or time								
Leg Abduction								
Leg Adduction								

Date	M	Tue	W	Th	F	Sat	Sun	Notes
Dying Bug								
Plank								
Side Plank								
Superman								
Knees— list # or time								
Short Arc Squat								
SLR								
Shoulders—list #								
Arm Raises								
Lateral/Front/Across								
External Rotation								
Internal Rotation								
Legs—List #								
Plantarflexion								
Dorsiflexion								
Inversion								
Eversion								
Wall Shin Raises								
Heel Step Downs								
E—equilibrium: daily								
Stork								
Toe Raise								
Hip Flexors								
Single Leg Raise								
Walk the Line								
CHOP								
Cone Touch								

By the end of six weeks, you will feel really different from the way you did when you started—I promise. Your body will feel stronger, your mind will be more confident, and you may even begin to look forward to the adrenaline rush that is a part of aerobic exercise. Changing your life does not happen overnight. It is a strategic commitment. Your body will change after a month or six weeks of working, so stay focused and don't lose heart.

If the six-week plan charted in Table 3 works for you, use it. My goal, however, is that you will *own* your future by planning strategically for it. *Make your own plan*. Copy the table on page 235, fill it in, and hang it on the refrigerator door.

As you finish a daily workout and feel some part of it went especially right or especially wrong, make a note of it. Not only is it fun to look back over the road you have traveled but the information can help you with your next plan.

At the end of six weeks, evaluate how you are doing:

- How do you feel while exercising?
- Do you need to rearrange your schedule to make it work for you?
- Do you have any injuries?
- Are there any barriers, mental or physical, that you need to work through?

When you have evaluated your first six weeks, make a second six-week plan toward your 12-week goal. As we discussed in Chapter 5, in order improve, you need to overload your body and make it work harder. In the next plan, covering Weeks 6–12, you need to increase the frequency, intensity, or time (duration) of your workouts to move to the next level.

To ramp up in the second 12 weeks from walking to running (if that is your goal), try fartlek training, which is a simple method

My Six-Week Plan for Getting off the Couch and onto My Future

	Monday	Tuesday	Wednesday	Thursday	Friday	Saturday	Sunday	Goal
Week 0								
Week 1								
Week 2								
Week 3								
Week 4								
Week 5								
Week 6								

F = flexibility (Chapter 4), A = aerobic (Chapter 5), C = carry a load (Chapter 6), E = equilibrium (Chapter 7) of alternating walking and running. First you start with a 5–10 minute walk, followed by a five-minute run. Continue alternating walking and running for a minimum of 20 minutes. Over the next several weeks, decrease the time you walk and increase the time you run until you can run for 20 to 30 minutes without stopping. When you can do that, you can simply ramp up your workouts by increasing your running times. You can also increase your intensity by keeping the total amount of time the same but running at a faster pace. If you want good race training schedules, there are many on the Internet, but I always use those designed by Hal Higdon at *www.halhigdon.com*. He makes schedules for all levels of runners and I have used them for all of my races.

If your goal is a sport other than running, you can also ramp up your workouts by increasing the frequency, distance, or intensity.

It is so exciting for me to think about you doing this because I know this is life-changing stuff. It makes me so happy to hear my patients tell me, in excited voices, the stories of their progress. I see the confidence in their faces and the swagger in their walk. You can do this. Onward!

HOME**WORK**

Take the time now to map out your six-week strategic plan. Use the table provided on page 229 to begin. You can go to *www.fitnessafter40book.com* for more examples of how to design your weeks. Make several copies of your plan and put them everywhere—in your car, on your mirror, on your computer, etc.—so the plan is always in front of you.

GLOSSARY

Achilles tendon injuries   A stretch, tear, or irritation to the tendon connecting the calf muscle to the back of the heel.

aerobic exercise   The physical activity that elevates the heart rate and breathing rate, thereby stimulating the cardiovascular system.

arrhythmia   An abnormally fast or slow heartbeat or an irregular heartbeat.

arthritis   The inflammation of a joint.

arthroscopy   The use of a small fiberoptic scope inserted through a small incision in the skin to see inside a joint.

ATP   Adenosine-5'-triphosphate, a compound used by cells for energy.

atrophy   The shrinking or wasting of an organ or tissue as a result of disease or lack of use.

BMI   See *body mass index*.

body mass index (BMI)   A measurement used to determine if a person's body weight is in the healthy range.

bone density   A measure of the amount of calcium and other minerals in bone in relation to the width of the bone.

bradycardia   A heart rate below 60 beats a minute.

bruise   An injury that results when muscle fiber and connective tissue are crushed; blood vessels may also be torn, taking on a bluish appearance. Most bruises are minor, but some can cause more extensive damage and complications.

cartilage   A type of connective tissue that is an important structural component of certain parts of the skeletal system such as the joints.

cold therapy   The use of ice packs to reduce inflammation by constricting blood vessels and limiting blood flow to the injured tissues; this eases pain by numbing the injured area. It is generally used for only the first 48 hours after injury. Also called *cryotherapy*.

compartment syndrome   A potentially serious medical condition. In many parts of the body, muscles (along with the nerves and blood vessels that run alongside and through them) are enclosed in a compartment formed of a tough membrane called fascia. When muscles become swollen, they can fill the compartment to capacity, causing interference with nerves and blood vessels as well as damage to the muscles themselves.

cool-down   The process of reducing the intensity of exercise at the end of a workout to help the body return to resting levels.

cryotherapy   See *cold therapy*.

dislocation   When two bones that come together to form a joint become separated.

duration   The amount of time a person spends doing a given exercise, whether it is aerobic exercise or strength training.

electrostimulation   The use of a mild electrical current to provide pain relief by preventing nerve cells from sending pain impulses to the brain.

fractures   Breaks in the bone that can occur from either a quick, one-time injury to the bone (called an acute fracture) or from repeated stress to the bone over time (a stress fracture).

frequency   How often a person does an exercise; for example, three times each week.

gastrocnemius   A muscle in the calf of the leg.

heat therapy   The use of heat, in the form of hot compresses, heat lamps, or heating pads, to cause blood vessels to dilate and increase blood flow to the injury site. Increased blood flow aids the healing process. Also called *thermotherapy*.

immobilization   A common treatment for sports injuries that may be done immediately by a trainer or paramedic. Immobilization involves reducing movement in the area to prevent further damage.

inflammation   Pain, swelling, and redness caused by immune cells in response to injury or autoimmune disease.

knee injuries   Problems with the knee that can range from mild to severe. Some of the less severe yet still painful and functionally limiting knee problems are runner's knee (pain or tenderness close to or under the kneecap at the front or side of the knee), iliotibial band syndrome (pain on the outer side of the knee), and tendonitis (also called tendinitis, marked by degeneration within a tendon, usually where it joins the bone). Knee injuries can result from a blow to or twist of the knee or from running too hard, too much, or without proper warm-up.

Krebs cycle   A series of chemical reactions, when oxygen enters a person's cells and becomes part of a miraculous and complicated energy-generating system.

massage   Manual pressing, rubbing, and manipulation to soothe tense muscles and increase blood flow to an injury site.

neurotrophic factor   A protein, such as nerve growth factor, that promotes nerve cell growth and survival.

non-steroidal anti-inflammatory drugs (NSAIDs)   A type of medication that doctors and other healthcare providers often recommend to reduce inflammation and pain. They are available over-the-counter (OTC) as aspirin, ibuprofen (Advil, Motrin IB, Nuprin), ketoprofen (Oruvail, Orudis), and naproxen sodium (Aleve). For more severe pain and inflammation, doctors may prescribe one of several dozen NSAIDs available in prescription strength. Like all medications, all NSAIDs can have side effects.

obesity   When a person's weight is 20 percent or more over the maximum desirable weight for his height, or body mass index is 30 or greater.

osteoarthritis   The most common type of arthritis, characterized by a degenerative process with inflammation around the joint.

rheumatoid arthritis   The most common type of inflammatory arthritis, usually affecting many joints, including the hands and feet.

shin splints   Pain along the tibia or shinbone, the large bone in the front of the lower leg. The term has been widely used to describe any sort of leg pain associated with exercise, but this is incorrect.

sprain   A stretch or tear of a ligament, the band of connective tissues that joins the end of one bone with another.

strain   A twist, pull, or tear of a muscle or tendon, a cord of tissue connecting muscle to bone. It is an acute, noncontact injury that results from overstretching or overcontraction.

tachycardia   A rapid heart rate, especially one above 100 beats per minute.

tendons   Strong, fibrous tissue that connects muscle to bone.

tendonitis   A degenerative condition caused by aging or overuse. When a tendon is weakened, trauma can cause it to rupture. Also called *tendinitis*.

thermotherapy   See *heat therapy*.

ultrasound   High-frequency sound waves used to produce deep heat that is applied directly to an injured area. Ultrasound stimulates blood flow to promote healing.

weight-bearing exercise   Any exercise, such as jogging, brisk walking, or stair climbing, that works the large muscles of the lower body, stimulating bone growth and building bone density.

DR. WRIGHT'S FAVORITE ONLINE SITES

I am beginning this section with a list of my favorite online sites. The Internet holds a bounty of information on fitness. Whether you are looking for instruction, scientific articles, or a source of equipment or want to have a talk with other active agers, there is a site for you. Here are a few of the sites that I especially like.

- fitnessafter40book.com
- www.masters-athlete.com: *Masters Athlete Magazine*, a great magazine specifically for masters athletes
- www.racenation.com: RaceNation, a premier race site
- www.aaos.org: American Academy of Orthopaedic Surgeons
- www.sportsmed.org: American Orthopaedic Society for Sports Medicine
- www.icaa.cc: International Council on Active Aging
- www.longlifeclub.com: Long Life Club, a great news site for living long

- home.hia.no/%7Estephens: Masters Athletes Physiology & Performance
- www.nsga.com: National Senior Games Association
- www.body1.com: Body1.com, a site where the Internet meets healthcare
- www.seniorsportsandfitness.com: Senior Sports and Fitness, my own website
- www.cdc.gov/nccdphp/dnpa/physical/measuring/target_heart_rate.htm: CDC's physical activity for everyone: measuring physical intensity
- www.fitness.gov/nolanryan.pdf: President's Council on Physical Fitness and Sports—the Nolan Ryan Fitness Guide

HELPFUL ORGANIZATIONS AND PUBLICATIONS

American Academy of Orthopaedic Surgeons (AAOS)
6300 North River Road
Rosemont, IL 60018
847-823-7186; fax 847-823-8125
www.aaos.org

The American Academy of Orthopaedic Surgeons provides education and practice management services for orthopedic surgeons and allied health professionals. It also serves as an advocate for improved patient care and informs the public about the science of orthopaedics.

American College of Rheumatology (ACR)
1800 Century Place, Suite 250
Atlanta, GA 30345
404-633-3777; fax 404-633-1870
www.rheumatology.org

The ACR is the professional organization of rheumatologists and associated health professionals who share a dedication to healing, preventing disability, and curing the more than 100 types of arthritis and related disabling and sometimes fatal disorders of the joints, muscles, and bones.

American College of Sports Medicine
401 West Michigan Street
Indianapolis, IN 46202
317-637-9200; fax 317-634-7817
www.acsm.org

The ACSM is a national organization of physical therapists, exercise physiologists, athletic trainers, and fitness professionals. They provide guidance for all aspects of fitness and sports health, set standards for exercise prescription, and certify personal trainers.

American Council on Exercise (ACE)
4851 Paramount Drive
San Diego, CA 92123
858-279-8227, 888-825-3636; fax 858-279-8064
www.acefitness.org

The American Council on Exercise provides a search engine on its website that can help you locate a certified exercise professional in your area. ACE is the largest sports medicine and exercise science organization in the world. Nearly 18,500 members throughout the United States and the world are dedicated to promoting and integrating scientific research, education, and practical applications of sports medicine and exercise science to maintain and enhance physical performance, fitness, health, and quality of life.

American Dietetic Association (ADA)
120 South Riverside Plaza, Suite 2000
Chicago, IL 60606

800-877-1600
www.eatright.org

The American Dietetic Association's website features comprehensive
nutrition information for the public, including a database of dieticians
in your area.

American Heart Association
7272 Greenville Avenue
Dallas, TX 75231
800-242-8721
www.americanheart.org

The American Heart Association's mission is to build healthier lives,
free of cardiovascular diseases and stroke. The AHA serves the public
and healthcare professionals alike by raising money for cardiovascular
research, providing community education, and raising the public's
awareness of cardiovascular health. For information on "Physical
Activity in Your Daily Life," check this part of the website:
www.americanheart.org/presenter.jhtml?identifier=2155.

American Medical Society for Sports Medicine (AMSSM)
11639 Earnshaw
Overland Park, KS 66210
913-327-1415; fax 913-327-1491
www.amssm.org

The society fosters relationships among sports medicine specialists and
provides educational resources for members, other sports medicine
professionals, and the public.

American Orthopaedic Society for Sports Medicine
6300 North River Road, Suite 500
Rosemont, IL 60018

847-292-4900; fax 847-292-4905
www.sportsmed.org

The society is an organization of orthopaedic surgeons and allied
health professionals dedicated to educating healthcare professionals
and the public about sports medicine. It promotes and supports educational and research programs in sports medicine, including those
concerned with fitness, as well as programs designed to advance
knowledge of the recognition, treatment, rehabilitation, and prevention of athletic injuries.

American Pain Foundation (APF)
201 North Charles Street, Suite 710
Baltimore, MD 21201
888-615-7246
www.painfoundation.org

The American Pain Foundation is a nonprofit information resource
and patient advocacy organization serving people with pain. Its mission is to improve the quality of life of people with pain by providing
practical information for patients, raising public awareness and
understanding of pain, and advocating against barriers to effective
treatment.

American Physical Therapy Association
1111 North Fairfax Street
Alexandria, VA 22314
703-684-2782, 800-999-2782; fax 703-684-7343
www.apta.org

The association is a national professional organization of physical
therapists, physical therapist assistants, and physical therapy students.
Its objectives are to improve physical therapy practice, research, and
education to promote, restore, and maintain optimal physical function,

wellness, fitness, and quality of life, especially as it relates to movement and health.

American Senior Fitness Association
P.O. Box 2575
New Smyrna Beach, FL 32170
888-689-6791; fax 386-427-0613
www.seniorfitness.net

The ASFA is a good resource for personal trainers and physical therapists to gain information and training for working with seniors. They publish a magazine called *Mature Fitness* that summarizes the latest training techniques and research.

Arthritis Foundation
P.O. Box 7669
Atlanta, GA 30357
800-283-7800
www.arthritis.org

The mission of the Arthritis Foundation is to improve lives through the prevention, control, and cure of arthritis and related diseases by providing grants to researchers to help find a cure, prevention, or better treatment for arthritis. The website provides links to information about different conditions, treatments, community groups, and more.

International Council on Active Aging
3307 Trutch Street
Vancouver, BC, Canada V6L-2T3
604-734-4466, 866-335-9777; fax 604-708-4464
www.icaa.cc

The International Council on Active Aging is dedicated to changing the way people age by uniting professionals in the retirement, assisted living, fitness, rehabilitation, and wellness fields to dispel society's myths about aging. The council helps these professionals to empower aging baby boomers and older adults to improve their quality of life and maintain their dignity.

International Society for Aging and Physical Activity
c/o Wojtek Chodzko-Zajko, PhD
ISAPA President
Department of Kinesiology
University of Illinois at Urbana-Champaign
Louise Freer Hall
906 S. Goodwin Avenue
Urbana, IL 61801
217-244 0823; fax 217 244-7322
www.isapa.org

The mission of ISAPA is to promote physical activity, exercise science, and fitness in the health and well-being of older persons and to promote international initiatives in research, clinical practice, and public policy in the area of aging and physical activity. The society organizes a World Congress on Aging and Physical Activity approximately every four years.

Lifelong Fitness Alliance
658 Bair Island Road, Suite 200
Redwood City, CA 94063
650-361-8282; fax 650-361-8885
www.50plus.org

The Lifelong Fitness Alliance works for lifelong wellness and seeks to teach people the benefits of physical activity. The group frequently holds events in various locations covering seminars, fitness activities, nutrition, and more for all adults.

Masters Athlete
www.masters-athlete.com

This is the first monthly magazine dedicated to masters athletes and
the games they play. At this website, you can also join discussion
boards about the broad range of masters sports and get extensive
masters sports calendars, downloadable e-books about masters sports,
and breaking news from the world of masters sports. You can also access *geezerjock.com*, which has special online-only content, e-newslet-
ters, and more.

National Senior Games Association
P.O. Box 82059
Baton Rouge, LA 70884
225-766-6800; fax 225-766-9115
www.nsga.com/directory.html

The association is a not-for-profit member of the United States
Olympic Committee dedicated to motivating senior men and women
to lead a healthy lifestyle through the senior games movement. The
organization governs the National Summer Senior Games, the largest
multi-sport event in the world for seniors, and other national senior
athletic events. It is also an umbrella for member state organizations
across the United States that host State Senior Games or Senior
Olympics.

National Athletic Trainers' Association
2952 Stemmons Freeway
Dallas, TX 75247
214-637-6282; fax 214-637-2206
www.nata.org

The association enhances the quality of healthcare for athletes and those engaged in physical activity. It also advances the profession of athletic training through education and research in the prevention, evaluation, management, and rehabilitation of injuries.

Senior Sports and Fitness.com
www.seniorsportsandfitness.com
Vonda J. Wright, MD
email: drwright@seniorsportsandfitness.com

This is my own website, where you can find information about my three-tiered approach, which focuses on improving the athletic performance of senior athletes, preventing the loss of independence in sedentary seniors through exercise, and promoting the use of physical exercise to improve the fiscal condition of the healthcare system.

Vegetarian Resource Group (VRG)
P.O. Box 1463, Dept. IN
Baltimore, MD 21203
410-366-VEGE
www.vrg.org

The Vegetarian Resource Group is a nonprofit organization dedicated to educating the public on vegetarianism and related issues. "Eat Better, Perform Better: Sports Nutrition Guidelines for the Vegetarian," by Enette Larson, MS, RD, can be found at the group's website at *www.vrg.org/nutshell/athletes.htm*. It provides guidelines for all types and levels of vegetarian athletes.

Women's Sports Foundation
1899 Hempstead Turnpike, Suite 400
East Meadow, NY 11554

516-542-4700, 800-227-3988; fax 516-542-4716
womenssportsfoundation.org

This is one of the most complete websites for female athletes, both
rookies and seasoned veterans. It has resources to help you play at
the top of your games, as well as descriptions of more than 100 sports
and fitness activities.

SELECTED REFERENCES

American College of Sports Medicine Position stand. "The recommended quantity and quality of exercise for developing and maintaining cardiorespiratory and muscular fitness, and flexibility in healthy adults." *Med Sci Sports Exerc.* 31(6): 916–920 (1999).

Beim, Gloria, and Winter, Ruth. *The Female Athlete's Body Book: How to Prevent and Treat Sports Injuries in Women and Girls* (McGraw-Hill, 2003).

Brandy, W. D., and Irion, J. M. "The effect of time on static stretch on the flexibility of the hamstring muscles." *Phys Therapy* 74: 845–852 (1994).

Brandy. W. D., et al. "The effect of duration of stretching of the hamstring muscle group for increasing range of motion in people 65 years or older." *Physical Therapy* 81(5): 1110 (2001).

Brandy, W. D., et al. "The effect of static stretch and dynamic range of motion training on flexibility for the hamstring muscles." *J Orthop Sports Phys Ther* 27(4): 295–300 (1998).

Campbell, W. W., and Geik, R. A. "Nutritional considerations for the older athlete." *Nutrition* 20(7–8): 603–608 (July–August 2004).

Chen, A., et al. "Orthopaedic Care of the Aging Athlete." *J Am Acad Orthop Surg* 13(6): 407–416 (October 2005).

Convertino, V.A., et al. American College of Sports Medicine Position Stand. "Exercise and Fluid Replacement." *Med Sci Sports Exerc* 28: R1–7 (1996).

Ferreira, Gustavo Nunes Tasca, et al. "PT Gains in Flexibility Related to Measures of Muscular Performance: Impact of Flexibility on Muscular Performance." *Clinical Journal of Sport Medicine* 17(4): 276–281 (July 2007).

Fontera, Walter R., et al. "Skeletal muscle fiber quality in older men and women." *Am J Physiol Cell Physiol* 279(3): C611–C618 (September 2000).

Katzel , Leslie I., Sorkin, John D., and Fleg, Jerome L. "A Comparison of Longitudinal Changes in Aerobic Fitness in Older Endurance Athletes and Sedentary Men." *Journal of the American Geriatrics Society* 49(12): 1657–1664 (2001).

Korhonen, Marko T., et al. "Aging, muscle fiber type, and contractile function in sprint-trained athletes." *J Appl Physiol* 101: 906–917 (2006).

Maharam, L. G. "Masters Athletes: Factors Affecting Performance." *Sports Medicine* 28(4): 273–285 (October 1999).

Maron, B. J., et al. "Recommendations for Pre-participation Screening and the Assessment of Cardiovascular Disease in Master Athletes." *Journal of the American Heart Association* 103: 327–334 (2001).

Mosekilde, Lise. "Age-related changes in bone mass, structure, and strength—effects of loading." *Journal Zeitschrift für Rheumatologie* 59(Supplement 1): I1–I9 (2000); also *Rheumatol* 59(1): 1–9 (2000).

Pyron, Martha I. "The aging athlete: Risks and benefits of exercise." *Sports Medicine* 13(2): 128–133 (April 2002).

Ryan, Nolan, and Jenkins, Jerry B. *Miracle Man: Nolan Ryan the Autobiography* (W Pub Group, 1993).

Ryan, Nolan. *Nolan Ryan Fitness Guide* (President's Council on Physical Fitness and Sports, Department of Health and Human Services, 2004).

Ryan, Nolan, and House, Tom. *Nolan Ryan's Pitcher's Bible: The Ultimate Guide to Power, Precision, and Long-Term Performance* (Fireside, 1991).

Ribisl, Paul M. "Clinical Applications: Toxic 'Waist' Dump: Our Abdominal Visceral Fat." *ACSM'S Health & Fitness Journal* 8(4): 22–25 (July–August 2004).

Rosenbloom, C. A., and Dunaway, A. "Nutrition recommendations for masters athletes." *Clinics in Sports Medicine* 26: 91–100 (2007).

Shaw, Jonathan. "The Deadliest Sin. From survival of the fittest to staying fit just to survive: Scientists Probe the Benefits of Exercise—and the Dangers of Sloth." *Harvard Magazine* (March–April 2004).

Sowers, MaryFran R., et al. "Sarcopenia is Related to Physical Functioning and Leg Strength in Middle Aged Women." *The Journals of Gerontology Series A: Biological Sciences and Medical Sciences* 60: 486–490 (2005).

"Sports Injuries." U.S. Department of Health and Human Services, National Institutes of Health, National Institutes of Arthritis and Skin Diseases. NIH Publication No. 04–5278 (April 2004).

Tanaka, H., and Seals, D. R. "Dynamic exercise performance in masters athletes: Insight into the effects of primary human aging on physiological functional capacity." *Journal of Applied Physiology* 95: 2152–2162 (2003).

Taylor, Dean, et al. "Vescoelastic properties of muscle-tendonitis: The biomechanical effects of stretching." *American Journal of Sports Medicine* 18: 300–309 (1990).

"Visceral Fat Build-up Is the High Cost of Inactivity," *Science Daily* (14 September 2005); www.sciencedaily.com/releases/2005/09/050914090337.htm, accessed 20 March 2008.

Willy, R. W., et al. "Effect of cessation and resumption of static hamstring muscle stretching on joint range of motion." *J Orthop Sports Phys Ther* 31(3): 138–144 (2001).

Wright, Vonda J. "Osteoporosis in Men." *J Am Acad Orthop Surg* 14: 347–353 (2006).

Wright, Vonda J., and Perricelli, Brett C. "Age-Related Rates of Decline in Performance Among Elite Senior Athletes." *American Journal of Sports Medicine* 36: 443–450 (May 2008).

INDEX

"Independent" fitness category, 37, 38
inflammation
  with arthritis, 153
  definition of, 239
  from injuries, 139
  NSAIDs for, 142, 152–153
injections, for arthritis, 155
injuries, *xvii–xx,* 135–150, 159
  acute, 144
  chronic, 144
  from cycling, 148–150
  flexibility for prevention of, 45
  healing from, 139
  increase in, 136
  from lack of flexibility, 43
  in masters athletes, 137–138
  mental training to deal with, 207
  precautions against, 136
  preventing/minimizing effects of, 100
  from running, 143–148
  and stiffening of muscles, 22
  from swimming, 148
  treating, 140–143
  of weekend warriors, 135–136
inspiration for exercise, 70
Institute of Medicine, National Academy of Sciences, 180
insulin sensitivity, 96
intensity of workout, target heart rate and, 79–80
International Council on Active Aging (ICAA), 222, 248–249
International Society for Aging and Physical Activity (ISAPA), 249
inversion/eversion, 115–116
investing in yourself, 9
iron

function of and intake recommendation for, 190
  in vegetarian diets, 196–197
Irongeezers, 2–3
Ironman Triathlons, 4
ISAPA (International Society for Aging and Physical Activity), 249
ITB syndrome, in runners, 144

joint bracing, for arthritis, 155–156
joint lubrication injections, for arthritis, 155
joint replacement, 161–168
  issues to consider for, 162–164
  Pre-hab for, 168
  rehabilitation after, 166
  results of, 164–165
  sports participation after, 167
  surgical procedure for, 166
joints
  arthritis in, 151–158
  and exercise economy, 25
  pain in, *xx*
Jonsson Cancer Center (UCLA), 74
The Journal of Applied Physiology, 30
Journal of the American Medical Association, 177

Kennedy, John F., on physical fitness, 200
Kimball, Aimee, 203, 207–208
kneecap, 145
knee injuries, 136
  in cyclists, 149–150
  definition of, 239
knees
  arthritis in, 123, 165–166, *see also* arthritis
  decrease in motion of, 25
  Fitness to Go workout for, 107–110

replacement of, *see* joint replacement
  tendonitis in, 28
Kolata, Gina, 89
Krebs cycle
  definition of, 239
  description of, 68

lactate threshold, 15
lactic acid, 15
  from anaerobic exercise, 78
  as muscle waste, 68
Larson-Meyer, Enette, 194
latissimus dorsi, 99
LDL (low density lipoprotein)
  as cardiac risk factor, 76
  lowering level of, 71
lean muscle mass, 22, 94
Leaves of Grass (Walt Whitman), *xxviii*
leg abduction, 102
leg adduction, 103
legs
  calves stretch for, 60–62
  Fitness to Go workout for, 113–118
  hamstring stretch for, 57–59
  injury of, 136
  quadriceps stretch for, 59–60
  tendonitis in, 28
leukocytes, 139
Lifelong Fitness Alliance, 249
life skills, 207
lifestyle
  inactive, *see* sedentary lifestyle
  to reduce cancer deaths, 73, 74
ligaments
  healing of, 139
  injuries to, 123
  stiffening of, 22, 25
liver, 180
low density lipoprotein, *see* LDL

VONDA WRIGHT

Vonda Wright, M.D., M.S., is an orthopaedic surgeon, speaker, author, and researcher working to maximize the fitness and performance of athletes over 40, from week-end warriors to elite competitors, while assisting them to remain injury-free. A valuable resource on healthy aging and orthopaedic issues, Dr. Wright is frequently quoted in the *Wall Street Journal*, *New York Times*, *U.S. News & World Report*, *USA Today*, CNN.com, and MSNBC and in magazines such as *Maxim*, *Best Life*, *Runner's World*, *Prevention*, and *Arthritis Today*. She has appeared on ABC Health News, NBC Nightly News with Brian Williams, and CBS affiliate KDKA-TV's Pittsburgh TODAY Live. Dr. Wright serves on the medical advisory board of the National Arthritis Foundation and *www.RaceNation.com*, a premier Web-based racing site.

In addition to caring for masters athletes and active agers, Dr. Wright performs research on musculoskeletal aging and stem cell tissue engineering for aging tendons. She directed the research conducted at the 2005 National Senior Olympics held in Pittsburgh, Pennsylvania.

Dr. Wright completed medical school at the University of Chicago Pritzker School of Medicine, her orthopaedic surgery residency at the University of Pittsburgh, and a fellowship in sports medicine and shoulder at the Hospital for Special Surgery in New York City. Currently practicing at the University of Pittsburgh Medical Center (UPMC), Dr. Wright specializes in sports medicine and is the director of PRIMA: the Performance and Research Initiative for Masters Athletes. In these roles, she cares for patients with a variety of musculoskeletal injuries.

A masters athlete herself, Dr. Wright runs road races from the 5K distance to marathons.

RUTH WINTER

Ruth Winter is an award-winning science writer who has written hundreds of magazine articles and 37 popular health books. She has won many awards including The Career Achievement Award from the American Society of Journalists and Authors (ASJA), The Article Writing Award from The American Medical Writers Association, the Service Award from the National Association of Science Writers, and The Golden Triangle Award from the American Academy of Dermatology. She has published pieces in *Woman's Day, Family Circle,* and *Good Housekeeping,* among other publications. Former Science Editor of the *Star-Ledger* in New Jersey and nationally syndicated columnist for *The Los Angeles Times,* she specializes in writing about scientific subjects that she makes understandable and interesting to the public. She is married to Arthur Winter, M.D., Director of The New Jersey Neurological Institute in Livingston, New Jersey, and has three children, Robin Winter-Sperry, M.D.,

CEO of Scientific Advantage LLC and its subsidiary MSL Advantage; Craig Winter, an executive with the Motion Picture Association of America; and Grant Winter, President of Manhattan Bureau LLC, a video production company. The Winters also have three grandchildren, Samantha, Hunter, and Katelynd. The Winters's website is brainbody.com.